MARGARET RIZZO MCKELVY
Diagrams by Onawa Rock

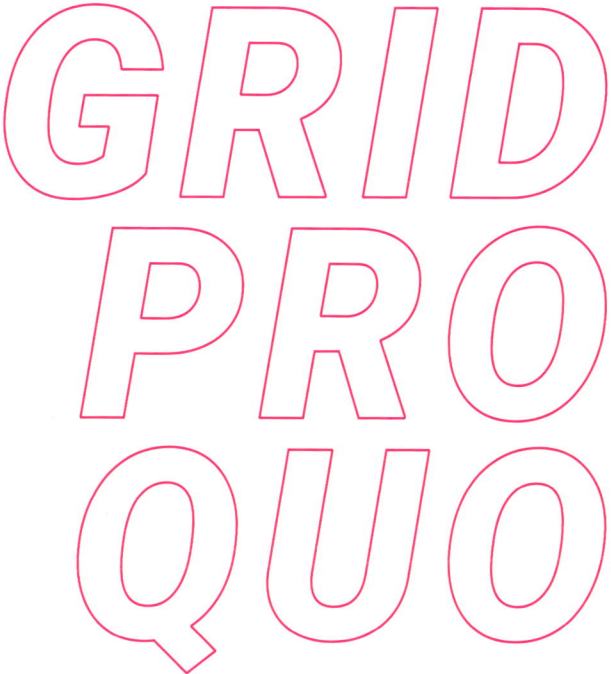

52 Powerful Jumping Exercises from the World's Top Riders

First published in 2022 by
Trafalgar Square Books
North Pomfret, Vermont 05053

Copyright © 2022 *Margaret Rizzo McKelvy*

All rights reserved. No part of this book may be reproduced, by any means, without written permission of the publisher, except by a reviewer quoting brief excerpts for a review in a magazine, newspaper, or website.

Parts of this book have been previously published in some form by *Eventing USA*.

Disclaimer of Liability
The author and publisher shall have neither liability nor responsibility to any person or entity with respect to any loss or damage caused or alleged to be caused directly or indirectly by the information contained in this book. While the book is as accurate as the author can make it, there may be errors, omissions, and inaccuracies.

Trafalgar Square Books encourages the use of approved safety helmets in all equestrian sports and activities.

Library of Congress Cataloging-in-Publication Data
Names: McKelvy, Margaret Rizzo, author.
Title: Grid pro quo : 52 powerful gymnastic exercises from the world's top
   riders / Margaret Rizzo McKelvy.
Description: North Pomfret, Vermont : Trafalgar Square Books, 2022. |
   Summary: "This modern-day quick reference to more than 50 grids and
   jumping exercises brings the best of top international training and
   instruction into your home ring. Build your skillset and your horse's
   confidence and conditioning with a fantastic selection of lessons
   contributed by the pros"-- Provided by publisher.
Identifiers: LCCN 2021031899 (print) | LCCN 2021031900 (ebook) | ISBN
   9781646010691 (hardback) | ISBN 9781646010707 (epub)
Subjects: LCSH: Jumping (Horsemanship)
Classification: LCC SF309.7 .M45 2022 (print) | LCC SF309.7 (ebook) | DDC
   798.2/5--dc23
LC record available at https://lccn.loc.gov/2021031899
LC ebook record available at https://lccn.loc.gov/2021031900

Diagrams by *Onawa Rock*
Book design by *Katarzyna Misiukanis–Celińska (https://misiukanis-artstudio.com)*
Cover design by *RM Didier*
Typefaces: *PT Serif* and *Roboto*

Printed in China

10 9 8 7 6 5 4 3 2 1

INTRODUCTION **1** THE EXERCISES **5** Michael **ALWAY** (US) **6** Laine **ASHKER** (US) **10** Tim **BOURKE** (IRE) **14** Stephen **BRADLEY** (US) **19** Molly **BULL** (US) **23** Jan **BYYNY** (US) **27** Daniel **CLASING** (US) **31** Sloane **COLES** (US) **35** Robert **COSTELLO** (US) **38** Sally **COUSINS** (US) **43** Phyllis **DAWSON** (US) **47** Martin **DOUZANT** (FRA) **51** Phillip **DUTTON** (US) **55** Will **FAUDREE** (US) **59** Sandy **FERRELL** (US) **64** Peter **FOLEY** (US) **69** Patty **FOSTER** (US) **72** Ariel **GRALD** (US) **75** Peter **GRAY** (CAN) **78** Sam **GRIFFITHS** (AUS) **82** Melissa **HUNSBERGER** (US) **85** Justine **JARVIS** (US) **89** Stephanie **JENKINS (NÉE RHODES-BOSCH)** (CAN) **92** Allison **KAVEY** (US) **96** Ingrid **KLIMKE** (GER) **99** Anne **KURSINSKI** (US) **102** Capt. John **LEDINGHAM** (IRE) **105** Mary Lisa **LEFFLER** (US) **108** Boyd **MARTIN** (US) **111** Caroline **MARTIN** (US) **116** Sinead **MAYNARD (NÉE HALPIN)** (US) **119** Tik **MAYNARD** (CAN) **124** Jenni **MCALLISTER** (US) **129** Margaret **MCKELVY** (US) **132** Heather **PARISH** (US) **136** Richard **PICKEN** (GBR) **139** Caroline **POWELL** (NZ) **143** Valerie **PRIDE (NÉE VIZCARRONDO)** (US) **146** Waylon **ROBERTS** (CAN) **150** Jenn **SCHUESSLER (NÉE SIMMONS)** (US) **155** Kim **SEVERSON** (US) **161** Brett **SHEAR-HEYMAN** (US) **165** Eric **SMILEY** (IRE) **169** Allison **SPRINGER** (US) **173** Sheryl **SUTHERBY** (US) **177** Meghan **TRUPPNER** (US) **181** Skyeler **VOSS** (US) **185** Danny **WARRINGTON** (US) **189** Whitney **WESTON** (US) **193** Sharon **WHITE** (US) **197** Kelley **WILLIAMS** (US) **200** Ryan **WOOD** (AUS) **204** ACKNOWLEDGMENTS **208**

CONTENTS

index

OF EXERCISES BY TYPE

◆ CAVALLETTI

Sandy Ferrell	64
Peter Foley	69
Justine Jarvis	89
Allison Kavey	96
Ingrid Klimke	99
Anne Kursinski	102
Boyd Martin	111
Caroline Martin	116
Jenni McAllister	129
Margaret McKelvy	132
Heather Parish	136
Waylon Roberts	150
Brett Shear-Heyman	165
Eric Smiley	169
Meghan Truppner	181
Ryan Wood	204

◆ COURSEWORK

Tim Bourke	14
Daniel Clasing	31
Sloane Coles	35
Phyllis Dawson	47
Phillip Dutton	55
Sandy Ferrell	64
Peter Gray	78
Melissa Hunsberger	85
Justine Jarvis	89
Anne Kursinski	102
Heather Parish	136
Richard Picken	139
Caroline Powell	143
Kim Severson	161
Brett Shear-Heyman	165
Allison Springer	173
Sheryl Sutherby	177
Skyeler Voss	185
Danny Warrington	189
Ryan Wood	204

◆ GROUNDWORK

Michael Alway	6
Martin Douzant	51
Tik Maynard	124

◆ TRADITIONAL GYMNASTIC

Laine Ashker	10
Tim Bourke	14
Stephen Bradley	19
Molly Bull	23
Jan Byyny	27
Robert Costello	38
Sally Cousins	43
Phyllis Dawson	47
Will Faudree	59
Patty Foster	72
Ariel Grald	75
Peter Gray	78
Sam Griffiths	82
Melissa Hunsberger	85
Stephanie Jenkins	92
Capt. John Ledingham	105
Boyd Martin	111
Sinead Maynard	119
Tik Maynard	124
Jenni McAllister	129
Margaret McKelvy	132
Valerie Pride	146
Waylon Roberts	150
Jenn Schuessler	155
Sheryl Sutherby	177
Danny Warrington	189
Whitney Weston	193
Sharon White	197
Kelley Williams	200

◆ TURNING

Laine Ashker	10
Daniel Clasing	31
Phillip Dutton	55
Mary Lisa Leffler	108
Caroline Powell	143
Kim Severson	161
Eric Smiley	169
Allison Springer	173
Meghan Truppner	181
Skyeler Voss	185

foreword

BY STEPHEN BRADLEY

Two-Time Gold-Medal Winner, Pan American Games
Land Rover Burghley Champion
Kentucky Three-Day Event Champion
US Olympic Committee Equestrian Athlete of the Year

As you all know, the partnership that develops between a horseperson and a horse is extremely important. It is developed through patience and time together, practicing and improving skills in groundwork, fitness, flatwork, and jumping. Getting to know your horse's personality, his physical strengths, weaknesses, and tendencies enables you to evaluate and put into practice the exercises and work needed to improve him. This will give your horse the best opportunity to be successful at whatever job he lets you know he wants to do.

I have known Margaret McKelvy for over a decade, both as an equestrian and as a successful businessperson. She is continually seeking out help and ideas to improve herself, her business, and her knowledge as a horseperson. This help comes through instruction both on and off her horses. She is well known and has written for numerous equine magazines, in particular her "Grid Pro Quo" column that was featured in *Eventing USA* for many years.

In her quest to learn, she has put together exercises from some of the top horsepeople in the world, including ground exercises, grids, and coursework. These are what make up this book, which is exceptionally written. Margaret helped each professional break down the exercises as to why they are necessary, what they develop, and how to execute them. She even addresses how to deal with challenges that might arise during each exercise. This book is an exceptional tool to add to anyone's toolbox in the search to better oneself as a trainer and partner to a horse.

Happy reading and good luck on your journey with your horse. ◆

introduct

GRID PRO QUO

INTR

introduction

My hope for this book is to put a year's worth of riding clinics into your hands. While I've been lucky to have regular instruction throughout my riding career, I know there is a large portion of the equestrian community that does not have the same access to training, whether due to location, finances, or schedules. This manual will put 52 lessons and plenty of new tools from our world's best riders and trainers at your fingertips.

As you flip through the pages you will see there is everything from basic cavalletti exercises, to complex footwork exercises, to flowing coursework exercises, to groundwork exercises. Simply put, there is something for every rider and every horse, regardless of discipline, level, or goals.

margaret rizzo mckelvy

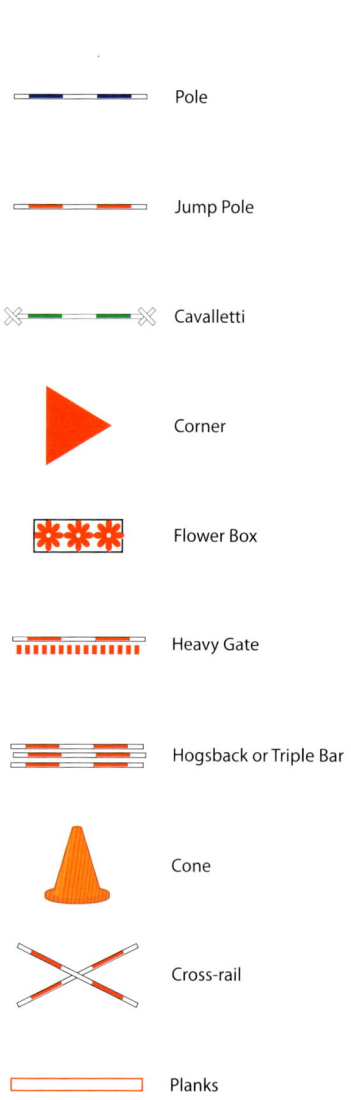

I have provided several easy ways to help you select an exercise for your schooling session. First, think about the space you have available. I've included exercises that are suited for small spaces, as well as ones that are best set in a larger arena. When you're looking at different exercises, remember that you should have a minimum of 20 feet between the first or last jump and the closest fence line. If your arena isn't big enough for your chosen exercise, you can either break the exercise up into pieces that fit your space or try setting it in a nearby field.

Next, think about the materials you have available. Included are exercises that range from a few ground poles to full courses of jumps. If you don't have everything you need for a particular exercise, get creative! Perhaps only set up part of the course, or maybe use cavalletti instead of jumps, or vice versa.

Finally, think about what you want to accomplish that day. Do you want to work on bending lines? Or footwork? Or maybe you want to try one of the unmounted exercises. Flip through the pages to see which diagram will best suit your needs for that particular day.

Every exercise starts with the name of the expert, what kind of exercise it is, a short summary, materials needed, and basic setup. Then the experts explain the "why" in their own voice: Why do they like a specific exercise, and why do they utilize it? Then, the experts move into the "how." How do they work through the exercise, step by step? You will find that this book also includes options to make each exercise simpler or more challenging. Again, there is something here for everyone.

GRID PRO QUO / *Margaret Rizzo McKelvy* /

Each exercise is illustrated with a basic diagram for setup and clear instructions for riding it. On the previous page, I have included a key that explains the various elements that may appear in the diagrams in the pages ahead.

For those readers who are inexperienced with setting courses, I encourage you to purchase a measuring tape or wheel. These are inexpensive and will help you immensely as you learn to set courses. Volunteering at your local horse show or assisting your instructor are also great ways to improve your course-setting skills.

Note: *The exercises ahead are organized in alphabetical order by expert. I have also included an index that lists the exercises by type on p. V.*

Don't be afraid to make notes in this book! I want it to be a tool that you can reference throughout your training. Consider these pages your own personal training diary. ◆

the exerci

GRID PRO QUO

EXERC

Michael **Alway** 6 Laine **Ashker** 10 Tim **Bourke** 14 Stephen **Bradley** 19 Molly **Bull** 23 Jan **Byyny** 27 Daniel **Clasing** 31 Sloane **Coles** 35 Robert **Costello** 38 Sally **Cousins** 43 Phyllis **Dawson** 47 Martin **Douzant** 51 Phillip **Dutton** 55 Will **Faudree** 59 Sandy **Ferrell** 64 Peter **Foley** 69 Patty **Foster** 72 Ariel **Grald** 75 Peter **Gray** 78 Sam **Griffiths** 82 Melissa **Hunsberger** 85 Justine **Jarvis** 89 Stephanie **Jenkins** 92 Allison **Kavey** 96 Ingrid **Klimke** 99 Anne **Kursinski** 102 Captain John **Ledingham** 105 Mary Lisa **Leffler** 108 Boyd **Martin** 111 Caroline **Martin** 116 Sinead **Maynard** 119 Tik **Maynard** 124 Jenni **McAllister** 129 Margaret **McKelvy** 132 Heather **Parish** 136 Richard **Picken** 139 Caroline **Powell** 143 Valerie **Pride** 146 Waylon **Roberts** 150 Jenn **Schuessler** 155 Kim **Severson** 161 Brett **Shear-Heyman** 165 Eric **Smiley** 169 Allison **Springer** 173 Sheryl **Sutherby** 177 Meghan **Truppner** 181 Skyeler **Voss** 185 Danny **Warrington** 189 Whitney **Weston** 193 Sharon **White** 197 Kelley **Williams** 200 Ryan **Wood** 204

EXPERT EXERCISE

Groundwork

Michael Alway

of Viewpoint Equestrian in Boyce, Virginia

▽ About the expert:

Michael specializes in starting horses, giving troubled horses a new start, trailer loading, behavior issues, developing solid foundations, and teaching horsemanship to anyone who wants to learn. He has helped Grand Prix dressage horses and riders, five-star eventers, international show jumpers, and amateur horse lovers alike. He studied natural horsemanship directly under Pat and Linda Parelli, spent time in Europe starting performance horses and learning from great horsemen, competed in Extreme Mustang Makeover events, and has started and restarted countless horses of different breeds and disciplines. All of this has taught him the importance of a solid foundation. His mission is to help educate and empower horse people and horses to become partners for performance. ◆

www.michaelalway.com

Whether your horse has never jumped before or is a seasoned competitor, this groundwork exercise will only improve his understanding of his job. While you don't need prior natural horsemanship experience, it's recommended that you do a little research on natural horsemanship techniques before trying this.

/ MATERIALS NEEDED

- 10- to 12-foot long obstacle (log, cavalletti)
- Rope halter
- 15- to 20-foot rope line
- Training stick

/ SETUP

- Set up your obstacle against a fence line. This can be done in an arena or in a field.
- Familiarize yourself and your horse with the rope halter, line, and training stick.

GRID PRO QUO / *Margaret Rizzo McKelvy* /

/ WHY

While some may be intimated by groundwork, it's something that I encourage all riders to explore. There are so many resources out there to educate yourself on proper groundwork techniques, and I encourage riders of all levels and disciplines to check them out.

When it comes to jumping, we all must first understand that unless a horse is micromanaged by his rider, he will typically choose to go around an obstacle, rather than over it. You can use this exercise to teach a horse to go out of his way to go over an obstacle, rather than around it.

This comes down to teaching the horse what his responsibility is, and to clearly explain your expectations to him. One of the benefits of first teaching this to a horse on the ground is that it easily transfers to under-saddle work, making a horse more likely to understand what his job is when there is a rider on his back.

Remember, a horse cannot be confident in his job until he understands it. When you teach your horse he can find comfort and reward by completing the chosen task, he will come to clearly understand his job, and be able to become confident in his job.

/ HOW

Before you start introducing your horse to jumping on the line, you do need to be able to complete two prerequisite tasks:

1. *Stand in one spot and be able to get your horse to back up without moving your feet.*

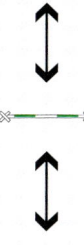

2. *Stand in place and be able to send your horse out on a circle in either direction, and specifically to yield the nose, neck, and shoulder out.*

When you're able to complete these prerequisites, you're ready to introduce your horse to jumping on the line.

To start, you want to position yourself about 5 feet from the base of the obstacle. This makes it harder for the horse to be able to go around it.

Then send your horse out on a circle and allow him to approach the log and acknowledge it. Your only goal here is for your horse to put his nose on the obstacle. Resist any temptation to chase your horse over the obstacle—that isn't the purpose here. The purpose is to get your horse to connect his brain to the obstacle, and reward him for that connection.

THE EXERCISES

Repeat this process until your horse is consistently putting his nose down to touch the obstacle. Whether your horse is on the hotter side or more laid back, this type of groundwork benefits all types. And should your horse have trouble focusing on and connecting with the obstacle, don't worry. Just keep repeating until your horse realizes that he gets a break (that is, a reward) when he acknowledges the obstacle. The goal for this first portion is for the obstacle to equal comfort.

After your horse is consistently and calmly acknowledging the obstacle, it's time to change your expectations. Now you want your horse to jump the obstacle, and to do this, you're going to show him that his comfort comes in the form of rest after completing the exercise.

You still don't want to chase your horse over the obstacle. Instead, you need to create impulsion on the first half of your circle, then leave your horse alone for the second half. Different horses need different levels of encouragement to create impulsion; some may simply need a cluck, while others need you to smack the ground with your training stick. Just be flexible in terms of what you do for your horse, and don't be afraid to adjust your own aids to match your horse's needs in that moment.

Remember, your attitude is, "It's no big deal if my horse jumps the obstacle or not." Horses learn nothing when they are in a stressed state, so the goal is to teach your horse something new in a relaxed and logical manner.

In most cases, your horse will likely jump the obstacle after a time or two with these new rules. When your horse does jump, be sure to reward him by bringing him in on the circle and giving him 30 to 60 seconds of stillness. This allows him to think and process, as well as get rid of any emotion or adrenaline that may have been created. Each horse is different and will require more or less "soak" time to process.

If your horse is still coming to a stop in front of the obstacle, you can do a few things to help him understand the new goal. First, remember you've changed the rules. Now, he doesn't get his reward until he has jumped the obstacle. So, keep your horse moving. If he comes to a stop in front of the obstacle, simply turn him away from it and approach it from the other direction, adding slightly more impulsion each time. Repeat this until he realizes he needs to try something new—that is, jumping the obstacle—to get a break. Once he realizes that the new answer is to go over the log, reward him with a break and allow him to process.

You should repeat this exercise at the same obstacle until your horse is jumping the obstacle with very little pressure from you.

If you are feeling confident in your skills here, you can do one of two things to increase the challenge. Your first option is to go to a new and different obstacle and start over. Or you can increase the space between you and the obstacle so that your horse now has an option to go around the obstacle. Both of these options are good ways to test your skills.

If you decide to increase the space between you and the obstacle, the obvious first desirable outcome is for your horse to continue to jump it. But, if he instead chooses to squeeze through the space between you and the jump, you want to create a moment of discomfort when he commits this mistake. For some horses, you can just smack the ground with your training stick, others may just need a shake of the training stick. Be sure that your level of intensity is just what you need to get a reaction.

Again, you will want to repeat this process until your horse decides to try something new, which in this case, is to go over the obstacle. Once your horse chooses this new answer, be sure to reward him by allowing him to rest until he is relaxed.

Generally speaking, it will not take long for a horse to develop a desire to jump. And that is the goal, for our horse to see a jump and think, "Yes, that's the answer." ◆

EXPERT EXERCISE

Traditional Gymnastic and Turning

Laine Ashker

of Laine Ashker Eventing and Dressage in Richmond, Virginia

▽ About the expert:

Based in Richmond, Virginia, Laine Ashker has built a business around teaching and training from the ground up. Laine takes pride in bringing up her horses herself. In addition to her busy competition schedule, Laine is busy teaching. She is a big believer in the power of positive reinforcement, which combined with a lot of patience, ensures that her students leave each lesson with a smile on their faces. ◆

www.laineashkereventinganddressage.com

Together these two exercises benefit both the horse and rider in slightly different but complementary ways. The horse is asked to compress and be quick, while the rider is asked to be still and strong.

/ MATERIALS NEEDED

- 4 ground poles
- 9 jump poles
- 9 sets of standards

/ SETUP

- If you are new to setting up bending lines, ask a more experienced person to help with Exercise 1.

- For Exercise 1, it's easiest to place your inside standards first and then lay out your poles and outside standards. Be sure to check both the inside *and* outside distances.

GRID PRO QUO / *Margaret Rizzo McKelvy* /

- For Exercise 2, it's easiest to place your jumps first and then your ground poles.

/ WHY

These are two of my favorite exercises for improving rider position and posture. I learned these both from my long-time coach Buck Davidson, and I utilize them often in the clinics I teach throughout the year.

One of the things I stress to my students is that they need to learn to do less. The less we do as riders, the better our horses will perform. If you stay balanced and in the middle of your horse, then he has one less thing to worry about and can instead worry about his own body. You'll notice that some of the best riders in the country could be considered the least interesting to watch because they are doing the least. These are the riders who are not interfering with their horses, and, therefore, their horses are able to keep a good rhythm throughout the course.

Of course, these riders put hours upon hours of training into making it look so easy! So on your journey to becoming the best rider you can be, I find these two exercises to be great!

Typically horses want to lengthen their stride to jumps, because they are eager to get there, because they are getting tired, or because their stride is getting flat. Exercise 1 is a typical "sharpening grid," but with a twist since the bounces are on a bending line. In Exercise 2, as the horse wants to lengthen, the distances get shorter and shorter, so your horse will either hit the rail or learn to compress and jump cleanly.

As a rider, it is your job to elevate your horse's shoulders to aid him in getting a clean round. When you are out of balance, your horse is more likely to knock a rail down. But in balance, your horse is more likely to be able to use his body most efficiently and leave the rails up.

PRO TIPS

- The close distance of the fences in Exercise 1, combined with the bending line, makes it quite easy to have a runout. If you warmed up correctly, you will have equal feel in both reins and your seat will be in the center of the saddle. When you've accomplished both these things, it should be easy to guide the horse through this bending line.

I always tell my students that I would rather they halted squarely in front of a jump a hundred times instead of having a runout. But if you do have a runout, the only way you'll be able to fix it is if you're able to halt correctly. So halt in front of the center of the rail and give your horse a pat. Repeat this as many times as necessary until your horse is quietly going to the center of the jump. Eventually your horse will realize that you are in charge, and if you choose to halt, you can choose to go straight through the exercise. The key to working through these issues is to REWARD, REWARD, REWARD!

THE EXERCISES

EXERCISE 1

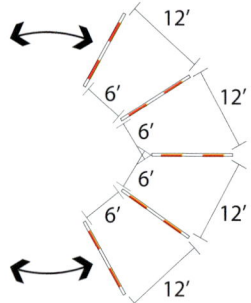

EXERCISE 2

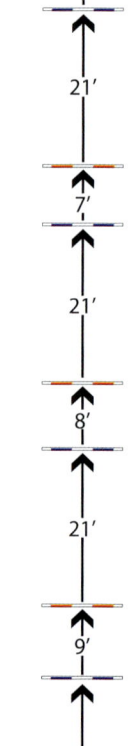

In the end, these grids will help you become less invasive, which will make for a faster, safer, and prettier ride.

/ HOW

Before heading toward your first jump, you should adequately warm up on the flat. Every horse is different, but the goal is to have a relaxed, balanced, and connected horse at the end of your warm-up.

Once you're properly warmed up, head straight to the fan of bounces (Exercise 1).

Greener horses and riders can start by walking and trotting through the fan of bounces as ground poles. This helps your horse get a feel for the exercise. From the very beginning you should be going from the middle of one rail to the middle of the next rail. You'll want to be looking in the direction that you're going and using a leading rein if necessary.

Once you've been through the rails a few times at the trot, pick up your canter and canter through a few times. Repeat the exercise in one direction before changing to the other direction.

For horses that have warmed up with the rails on the ground, or for more experienced horses, put the bounces in with alternating sides in the cups. This will help you find the center of each rail as you go through the exercise.

After a time or two through the exercise like this, raise both sides of the rails so they are now all verticals. But at no point should the verticals get any higher than a foot tall.

The biggest challenge for the rider in this exercise is keeping the horse straight!

GRID PRO QUO / *Margaret Rizzo McKelvy* /

These bounces really help to create a self-elevating canter, as well as a rhythmic, even canter stride. Your goal is to maintain the canter that the bounces create well after the exercise is over!

After you've completed this bounce exercise a few times and are working on successfully maintaining your quality canter afterward, move on to Exercise 2, the straight grid.

Start with all the rails on the ground and build up the exercise jump by jump. You'll want to keep all the jumps at or below your comfort level until you've built up the entire exercise. Know that the jumps will seem inherently bigger the closer you get to them. In general, horses give a more athletic effort to jump cleanly from a takeoff distance close to the ground line or base of the jump. Since this exercise is forcing your horse to get close to the jumps, don't make the jumps too big. If you want to raise a jump or two, raise the first and last vertical.

This is the perfect exercise for horses that like to rush a bit. Horses tend to rush because they're used to being held off the jumps.

As a rider, the poles are here to do all the work, so your job is to stay balanced and out of the way!

One trick for a rider/horse combination that has a tendency to rush is to come into the exercise a gear faster than you are used to. Because this exercise is so complex, your horse will have to slow down and think about his body in order to make it through without making a mess of the rails. This puts you in a win-win situation because your horse will learn to naturally slow down and then you can reward him for being good! And as I stated before, I'm a big believer in rewarding your horse for doing his job. ◆

EXPERT EXERCISE

Coursework and Traditional Gymnastic

Tim Bourke

of Stone's Throw Farm in Berryville, Virginia

▽ About the expert:

A native of Ireland, Tim Bourke has established himself as a top rider and sought-after trainer in the United States after two years of working for eventing legend Bruce Davidson and another six years with leading rider Sharon White. He has competed through the five-star level, including completions at Kentucky CCI5* and Burghley CCI5* with his longtime partner Luckaun Quality. He is currently based out of Stone's Throw Farm in Berryville, Virginia, which he runs with his wife Marley. ◆

www.bourkeeventing.com

This exercise is great for those needing to set up one exercise for multiple horse-and-rider combinations, or for someone who wants an exercise that can be utilized over a few jump schools. While there is a traditional gymnastic element to it, there are also several options for courses.

/ MATERIALS NEEDED

- 1 ground pole
- 11 jump poles
- 11 sets of standards

/ SETUP

- This requires an arena at least 130 feet long.
- Set up your centerline first, with the jump poles in place.

GRID PRO QUO / *Margaret Rizzo McKelvy* /

- Then set up Jump E in relation to Jump C, before setting Jump G.

- Then set Jump H in relation to Jump C, before setting Jump F.

- Once all your jumps are set, move all your poles to the side, except for the ground pole (blue in the diagram).

/ WHY

One of the challenges as an instructor is coming up with exercises that are appropriate for a wide range of horses and riders, and while at first glance this exercise can seem a bit complex and intimidating, it is actually perfect for horses and riders of all levels—from those just starting out jumping right on up through the highest levels. I borrowed the base of this exercise from my longtime coach Jimmy Wofford, and then made it a little different to suit the needs of both my own horses and my students' horses.

Another great thing about this exercise is that it is something you can leave set up in your ring for a few weeks and just build on with each jump school. I especially recommend this for the less experienced horses and riders, as I always prefer to end a jump session a little early rather than pushing yourself too much past your comfort zone and running into trouble.

With so many different options in this setup, it is easy to get overwhelmed, so I like to break things up into pieces. And if this means you need to break this up into a few different jump schools, that is fine.

On the other hand, if you're a more experienced pair, it can sometimes be good to push yourself a bit and play with all the different options in one jump school at a lower height, then come back the next time and challenge yourself with some bigger fences.

/ HOW

After you've finished your basic flat warm-up, start your jump school by trotting over the ground pole and through the entire set of standards on the centerline. You will want to approach this ground pole from each direction, but always go through the complete set of standards. Especially for greener horses, you want them to get the idea of always going straight through the

THE EXERCISES

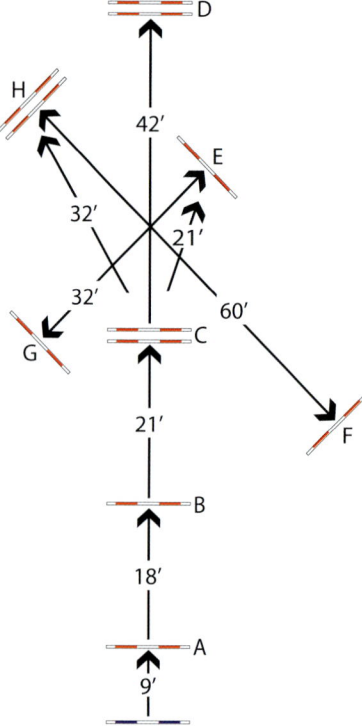

line after a jump. And for the less experienced riders, it's good to have a goal of staying straight on the landing side of the jump, as many riders tend to stop riding after they land. It's good to instill the basics early and often!

Once your horse is trotting quietly over the ground pole, you can add Jump A. Again, depending on your level this first jump can start out as a small cross-rail, or you can start with a small vertical. Now that you have a jump, don't change anything about how you're riding your horse. Keep the same forward trot that you had over the ground pole, look ahead through your line of standards, and ride forward and straight.

One thing to keep in mind is that there should be one full trot step between the ground pole and Jump A. So, if your horse is taking off a bit early, simply sit up taller, steady your trot, and give your horse every opportunity to make the right decision with his footwork.

If your horse is really trying to rush now that there is a jump in place, you can always come to a halt after this first jump. Ideally, you would be able to halt before the set of standards for Jump C, but if your horse is really trying to run off, this can be your goal that you work toward for your first jump session. Then you can come back to the exercise the next day.

On the flip side, if your horse is slowing down between the ground pole and Jump A, then you know that you need to keep your leg on a bit more as you go over the ground pole. And if he is still slowing down, make sure that as you land over Jump A you really send him forward through the line of standards.

GRID PRO QUO / Margaret Rizzo McKelvy /

Assuming that your horse is jumping Jump A quietly and confidently, you can add Jump B. Unless the horse is really struggling with his straightness, I prefer Jump B to be a vertical. However, you know your horse best, so if you think that this should be another cross-rail, that's fine.

And the same goes for the remaining two oxers—Jumps C and D—on the centerline. While I prefer them to be traditional oxers, if horse or rider is really struggling with straightness, they can be cross-rail oxers, where the front set of standards is a cross-rail and the back set of standards a vertical. For the rider, more so than the horse, the cross-rails give a definite place to focus.

For greener horses and riders, this centerline gymnastic might be enough for the first day. For more advanced horses and riders, this is where all the work on straightness starts to pay off, because now you can start adding the bending lines. And everyone knows that before you start attempting bending lines, you need to make sure that your horse is straight between your aids.

However, with that said, a common problem with this exercise is that once you've done the centerline gymnastic a few times, the horse can get a little confused when you try to add in a bending line after Jump C. For this reason, I will often leave the outside jumps—Jumps E, F, G, and H—as ground poles for the first time through in each direction. Again, this is just one more way to set yourself, and more importantly, your horse up for success.

As an instructor, I often find that I have to remind my students to not only look where they want to go, but to also put their weight in the stirrup of the direction that they're going. Not only will your horse naturally want to follow the weight of the rider, but it also mentally gives him a clue as to which direction you want to go while you're approaching the preceding jump.

One of the great things about adding in the bending lines is that for the horses that were rushing at the beginning, this is the perfect way to get them to pay attention. And this is another reason why you always want to change which direction you're coming from and which direction you're going when you land. For most horses, this is enough to get them to really tune in to you and start listening. So then, it is up to you to give your horse the best ride possible to reward him for listening!

As you work through the centerline gymnastic and then the bending line exercises, you are looking for your horse to use his body effectively and efficiently. This is one of the reasons why you always approach the centerline gymnastic at the trot, because it is always much easier to get an accurate

THE EXERCISES

distance out of the trot than the canter. You also want to remember that it is your horse's job to jump the jump, so don't try to help him too much.

After you've successfully done the centerline exercise incorporating Jump H 32 feet to the left and Jump E 21 feet to the right, you can start to canter some single fences. My favorite course is to do the centerline gymnastic, bending right after Jump C to Jump E 21 feet away. Then canter left all the way around the ring and jump Jump F 60 feet to Jump H. And then you keep turning right and jump Jump E and G, which are 32 feet apart.

As you work through this exercise, whether it is in one day or over the course of several days, you need to look at yourself as a coach. If you start to have a runout, you know that you've made the exercise a little bit too challenging, too quickly. Most times, if a horse starts to really shut down it is because of a lack of understanding. Horses are not bad creatures by nature, so you need to keep that in mind and take a look at the situation you have put them in. You will need to take a step back and figure out where you got ahead of yourself. If this means that you have to put the jumps down to ground poles a few times through, that is completely fine! You want there to be an understanding between horse and rider. And sometimes breaking it down to the basics is what you need. ◆

EXERCISE

Traditional Gymnastic

EXPERT

Stephen Bradley

of Stephen Bradley Eventing in The Plains, Virginia

This traditional gymnastic is great for horses that want to rush or jump over their shoulders. And like any good trot gymnastic, it helps teach riders to stay balanced over their stirrups and allow their horses to do their job.

/ MATERIALS NEEDED

- 6 ground poles
- 15 jump poles
- 13 sets of standards

/ SETUP

- This exercise has two options, depending on your experience level and the space you have available.

- Set up your exercise completely and then take out all the poles except the four ground poles to get started (Exercise 1).

▽ About the expert:

Stephen Bradley's career as a professional equestrian has included accomplishments that reflect his focused dedication to eventing. He has been on two gold-medal-winning Pan American Games teams and has also placed in the Top 10 five times at Kentucky CCI5*. And he is only one of two American riders to win the Land Rover Burghley CCI5*, doing so in 1993 with Sassy Reason. Stephen is not just a competitor; he brings a wealth of horsemanship to his students and his team, and shares his expertise teaching all over the country. ◆

www.stephensbradley.com

EXERCISE 1

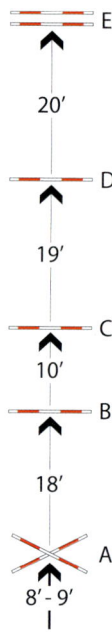

EXERCISE 2

/ WHY

I've been lucky to teach all over the country, which has been great for my growth as an instructor. One of the best things you can do as a rider is watch others as much as possible. Think about it—watching riders warm up at shows is free! And most clinics have a nominal auditing fee. So the next time you have a spare weekend, find a local show or clinic and spend a day watching. I bet you'll come away inspired to go home and practice what you learned.

This trot grid is one that I have developed over the years. Like most good grids, it is particularly helpful for quick horses and for those that want to jump over their shoulders. And it's a great exercise for ensuring riders stay balanced over their feet and not get ahead of their horses' center.

In addition to emphasizing all the things that any gymnastic emphasizes—straightness and footwork—this exercise really helps rebalance a horse that falls on his forehand. It demands that through the rebalancing, the horse keeps going forward. And the most important thing you can teach a horse is how to keep moving forward through the questions he might face.

/ HOW

Be methodical and build up the trot grid one fence at a time. After your horse has sufficiently warmed up on the flat, you should walk, then trot through three or four ground poles set 4 feet 6 inches apart (Exercise 1). This is just to get your horse thinking about where his feet are.

GRID PRO QUO / *Margaret Rizzo McKelvy* /

Then set up a small cross-rail as Jump A with a ground rail (see Exercise 2). After a few trips over the cross-rail, place another ground pole 8 to 9 feet in front of Jump A.

The final warm-up step is to raise the cross-rail (Jump A) to your maximum comfort level.

Your next fence will be Jump B, one stride from the cross-rail. For the first trip through, you want to leave Jump B low so your horse isn't surprised.

Then comes Jump C, which is placed 10 feet from Jump B. This completes your first bounce.

Early on in any grid, try to make the second fence (Jump B) fairly sizable (that is, at your maximum comfort level) to make sure that you have your horse in front of your leg. With this particular grid, for lower-level pairs (those jumping 3 feet and below), make Jump B larger before adding in Jump C. For higher-level pairs, wait until Jump C is in, then make that quite large.

After you've gone through the grid a few times with the raised vertical—whether that was Jump B or C—put it back down to a height more in line with what you're schooling.

You now have two options depending on your level. The lower levels have Exercise 2, which has a single bounce. The higher levels have an additional bounce, as illustrated as Jump F in Exercise 3. This extra bounce really makes horses and riders work. The horses have to remain light on their feet, while their riders must remain strong through their core.

After you've completed the bounce portion of the grid, you'll add your final vertical (Jump D).

And lastly, the final oxer (Jump E).

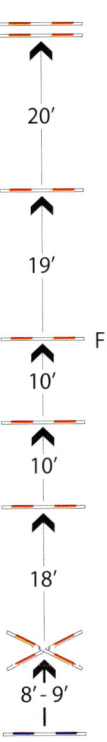

THE EXERCISES

After you've been through the complete grid at least twice, you can play with making Jump E larger, making it at or slightly above your competition height.

Remember that at this point horses have done a lot of work, so it wouldn't be fair to over tax them with a huge oxer, no matter how much fun it might be.

This is a great exercise to warm up over before practicing a few canter fences. ◆

EXERCISE

Traditional Gymnastic

EXPERT

Molly Bull

of MHB Event Organizing in Scottsville, Virginia

This is a great canter gymnastic that will help you develop the proper canter for a show jumping course. The repetitive nature of the jumps and the distances allows for riders to really work on their positions.

▽ About the expert:

Molly Bull is a Level II Certified Instructor through the USEA's ICP program. She has also competed through the five-star level and brought two horses from green prospects to the Advanced level. Molly and her husband, renowned course builder Eric Bull, have a young son, Henry. Molly is now focusing on being a mom, teaching lessons, and managing her event organizing business. ◆

/ MATERIALS NEEDED

- 4 ground poles (optional)
- 5 jump poles
- 5 sets of standards

/ SETUP

- Set up your jumps first, either on the centerline or quarterline of an arena, with all jump poles on the ground.

- Place your ground poles to the side. If you do need to utilize the ground poles, they should be placed directly in the middle of each set of verticals (10 feet 6 inches from each vertical).

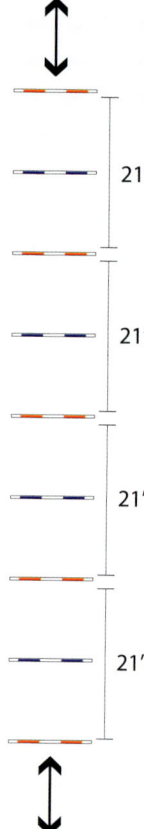

/ WHY

I utilize grids regularly in my day-to-day training, and while many of them are trot grids, it's nice to have exercises that you can canter into. And these five verticals make up one of my favorite canter grids. Since you're always cantering to your fences in competition, the regularity of this canter grid will help you develop your eye a bit. This way when you're at a competition you can take a deep breath and not worry about finding the perfect spot because you will have spent time schooling the right canter.

Unlike most trot grids, where the distances lengthen throughout, all five verticals in this exercise are set the same distance apart. For horses, this helps to teach them to hold the same canter throughout, while also helping to sharpen their footwork. For riders, the repetitive distances help them develop their eye. This exercise has so many variations that you can do it with almost any horse. I'll often leave it set up in my ring to go back to whenever I'm looking to help a horse or rider solidify their competition canter.

/ HOW

Depending on your level, you can start the exercise in one of two ways. When you are less experienced, leave all the rails on the ground and build it up from there. If you are more experienced, put all the verticals up at a very low height—maybe 2 feet—and go from there.

Let's start as if you're less experienced, and the more experienced reader can catch up with us once all the jumps are up.

GRID PRO QUO / *Margaret Rizzo McKelvy* /

To begin, put all the vertical rails on the ground and have your horse walk, trot, then canter through. Once your horse is cantering through the rails without a change in rhythm, put up the first vertical.

However, if you have a horse that is rushing through the rails on the ground, go ahead and add in additional ground rails between each set of standards. This ground rail should be placed directly in between where the verticals will be, so 10 feet 6 inches from each future vertical. Typically, this is all you need to do get an eager horse to pay attention.

Once you're cantering through the ground rails off both leads without loss of rhythm for your horse, or loss of position for yourself, you're ready to put in your first vertical. The best plan is to always add things in gradually. If your horse started off quietly and you didn't have to add in the additional ground rails to start, add your first vertical and canter over that and your subsequent rails where future verticals will be placed.

Add in the additional middle ground rails. Especially for green horses, this exercise is a lot to look at, so it's best to start off slowly versus skipping a step and causing trouble later on. If, for some reason, your horse starts to back off or lose confidence at any point, don't hesitate to take a step back and remove the ground rail or vertical that started the trouble. Continue to build the exercise back up. It's up to you whether you feel that your horse has regained enough confidence to continue, or whether you should call it a day once you've worked through your issue and come back another day.

As long as your horse is confidently jumping, continue to add one vertical or ground rail at a time until they are all in place. As I said before, this is not an exercise where you need to make the jumps really big. At most the jumps should be at your competition level, if not a little below.

If you're riding a green horse, or this is your first time doing this exercise, you will probably want to stop after you've gone through the completed exercise a few times. Then for your next jump school, you can start with all the jumps up at a low height and move on.

When you're a more experienced pair, start with all five verticals in place at a very low height—maybe 2 feet. This is just a nice little warm-up exercise to get the horse and rider's jump muscles moving.

Keep raising all the verticals two holes at a time until you reach your present comfort level or competition height. But the same rules apply for the experienced as for the greener pairs: do not add the next piece until you both are confidently completing what's in front of you.

If you are having trouble seeing a distance and keep trying to kick for the long one or holding for the chip, try raising the middle three fences. By keeping the first fence smaller, it helps to get you confidently into the exercise. Then the remaining verticals help show you where the correct takeoff spot should be.

If possible, set this exercise up on the centerline so that you can approach it from both directions, which is another reason to leave the first and last verticals lowered.

For the more experienced horse-and-rider combinations, you can use raised cavalletti instead of rails on the ground between the verticals. Most often, I will use the raised cavalletti between the first two and last two fences. This really helps to sharpen up the horse's form and make him think about where he is putting his feet.

For riders, this exercise is great for working on your position. Since the jumps are all the same distance apart, it's a good time to focus on keeping your shoulders tall, heels down, and elbows and hands in the right position. You'll find that this exercise teaches you to ride with a softer rein, which is especially good for horses that want to rush, or riders who want to hold their horses.

As you're working through this exercise, don't be surprised if your horse gets tired a little bit sooner than you were expecting. These verticals can wear him out because he is having to rock back a lot. I will sometimes just do this for the day or do a little coursework afterward if my horse worked through the exercise quickly. ◆

EXERCISE

Traditional Gymnastic

EXPERT

Jan Byyny

of Surefire Eventing in Purcellville, Virginia

This is a great exercise for teaching riders how to deal with a variety of distances, including the inevitable long distances. You will learn how to stay with your horse regardless of the distance you find, which will make you a well-rounded rider.

/ MATERIALS NEEDED

- 3 cavalletti
- 2 jump poles
- 2 sets of standards

/ SETUP

- Set this up in a place where you can approach it from either direction.

- It isn't a problem if you don't have cavalletti. You can use flower boxes or mini brick walls that add a degree of difficulty because of their narrow width. If you don't have any type of

▽ About the expert:

Owner of Surefire Farm in Purcellville, Virginia, Jan Byyny's focus is selecting, training, and competing event horses. She's represented the United States numerous times at home and abroad, and her career highlights include team gold and individual bronze at the Pan American Games, being a member of the Aachen World Equestrian Games squad, competing on the US Equestrian Team at Malmo, Sweden, and Luhmühlen, Germany, and being selected as a team alternate for the Athens Olympics. ◆

www.surefireeventing.com

cavalletti or boxes, you can simply use additional jumps set to a low height.

/ WHY

There are several reasons why I love this jumping exercise. While it looks simple on paper, it can be quite challenging when set up in your arena. It is also great for a variety of horses and riders, which is why I often use it when teaching. Over the years, I have found that a lot of riders are uncomfortable with a distance that is long or feels long, and subsequently end up out of balance.

Since it is impossible to have that "perfect distance" every time, this exercise is for practicing how to stay with the motion of your horse through a variety of distances. Additionally, the bounces work well for teaching riders how to move their hands forward independently, while staying nice and tall through their bodies.

The key to getting the most out of this exercise for your horse is to not help him too much. And like most riders, I can tell you that this is often the hardest thing to do! As a rider you have to create the right canter, and then trust that your horse can cover the distances. You'll need to focus on your own position so that you're able to let your horse figure things out on his own, without hindering him in any way.

For the green horse that is still working on learning how to go from a big, loose canter to a smaller canter, the 12-foot bounces will teach him how to rock back a bit and balance himself while still covering a long distance. Older horses will typically not have trouble with the bounces but will quickly remember that they need to be adjustable when they get into the 18-foot, one-stride verticals.

Finally, when setting up this exercise in your ring at home, try to place it in a spot where you can approach it from both directions. I think it's really important to be able to practice an exercise like this from both directions, as some horses are more confident on one lead than the other. It's best to practice exercises like this on both leads so you can work on your weaknesses, as this is the only way to get better!

/ HOW

Before you start jumping, you should work on your horse's rideability on the flat. Make sure you can easily and confidently send your horse forward and bring him back. You should also be able to turn in both directions while staying in balance and not changing the rhythm.

More advanced riders should challenge themselves to practice some lateral work and even a bit of counter-canter into their warm-up. The end goal for the warm-up session is to be able to go from a 12-foot canter to a 14-foot canter from your leg aid, then be able to shorten back to a 12-foot canter by simply sitting up and using your seat.

The more responsive and relaxed your horse is, the better chance he will jump a clean round. It is your job as rider to set your horse up for success, regardless of what you are doing. So this is why I put so much emphasis on a proper flat warm-up before jumping.

Depending on the experience level of the horse and rider, I start this exercise in a few ways. For a younger, less experienced horse or a lower-level rider, I would start in the following manner:

Start by putting Cavalletti A to the side, so that there is just the Cavalletti B with 12 feet to a small vertical (Jump C), and then the second vertical (Jump D) and Cavalletti E can be on the ground. This allows the horse and rider to get used to the distances, while establishing their rhythm so they can really attack the grid with confidence once all the pieces are put in place. Confidence, in both the horse and rider, is a huge part of this exercise, so I am always sure to take my time when setting up the pieces.

Once both the horse and rider are comfortable with this first part of the grid, add Cavalletti A to complete the double-bounce portion of the exercise. For more experienced horses, you can begin the exercise here, as a double bounce should not surprise a Training Level or above horse. However, for the younger horses, don't be surprised if they back off when they first see the additional cavalletti. As a rider, all you should do is put your leg on and encourage your horse to go confidently forward through the jumps.

Finally, add Jump D and eventually you can raise Cavalletti E. The final cavalletti is key for this grid, as it forces the horse and rider to "finish" the exercise. I often see riders collapsing in their positions when they think they are done with an exercise, so this forces them to stay tall and keep riding. For horses, this final cavalletti forces them to think about their scope, and not just rushing flat through the jumps.

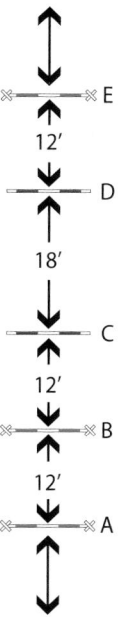

THE EXERCISES

While working through the exercise, I like to think about what the horse needs to work on when deciding on the fence height. When I'm working with a horse that isn't always the best about using his scope or figuring out how to back off the jumps, I raise the verticals rather quickly to his competition height. This really encourages horses to not jump past their distance and be smart with their feet. However, if I need to build confidence in the horse, I keep the verticals on the small side and concentrate on making sure he has a positive ride through the exercise.

Throughout the jump school, I work with my students to make sure they are maintaining their own balance so they are able to keep a steady contact with their horses' mouths. As riders it is our responsibility to let our horses do *their* jobs, and one of the most important jobs *we* have is setting a good rhythm. A good rhythm allows you to adjust your horse's stride so he can comfortably cover any distance you put in front of him. ◆

EXERCISE

Coursework and Turning

EXPERT

Daniel Clasing

of Clasing Equestrian in Lovettsville, Virginia

This is a great exercise for those with limited space or jumps. There is a lot that you can do with just four jumps!

/ MATERIALS NEEDED

- 6 jump poles
- 6 sets of standards

/ SETUP

- It is easiest to center this in your jumping arena or field.

- To set up your first line, find the center point of your arena and walk 36 feet toward the top right corner and place a jump pole on the ground to create the inside rail of Jump A. Then walk 36 feet from the center point to the bottom left corner and place another jump pole to create Jump C. And then double check that your total distance is 72 feet.

▽ **About the expert:**

Based in the heart of Area II eventing country, Daniel Clasing operates his training and teaching business in Lovettsville, Virginia, alongside his wife Kaitlin. Daniel prides himself in bringing horses along from the very beginning and has competed through the five-star level. He specializes in the correct development of young event horses and instills these basics in all his students as well. ◆

www.clasingequestrian.com

- To set up your second line, go back to your center point and walk 33 feet toward the top left corner and place a jump pole on the ground to create the inside rail of Jump D. Then walk 33 feet from the center point to the bottom right corner and place another jump pole to create Jump B. And then double check that your total distance is 66 feet.

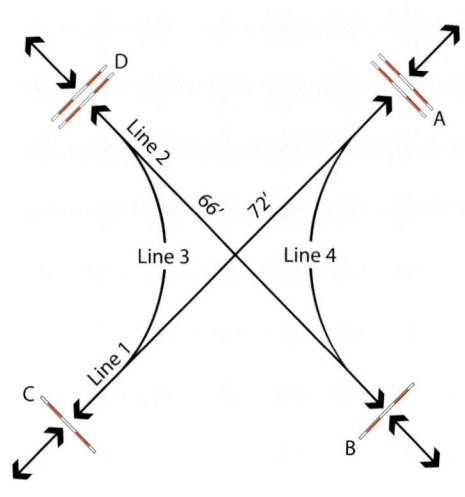

/ WHY

At first glance, this four-jump exercise may seem overly simple. But over the years, it has become one of my favorites for both my students and my own horses. The main reason why I keep using it over and over again is because it is so versatile. You can use this for horses and riders just starting out, all the way up to the most advanced pairs.

From a practical standpoint, it is also an easy exercise for riders to set up at their home rings. Depending on the size of your ring, you can play with the angles between the fences to make your bending lines easier or harder. You can even set this up out in a field so that the terrain adds a little bit of difficulty. You'd be really surprised at how creative you can be with just four jumps!

/ HOW

Before you even approach the first pole on the ground, you should accomplish a few things while warming up on the flat. Both of the straight lines in this exercise are meant to be ridden in five strides. This requires adjustability because one line measures 72 feet, while the other measures 66 feet. To help set your horse up for success, play with sending your horse forward then bringing him back within all three gaits while warming up.

Of course, the degree of change within the gaits is dependent on the level of the horse and rider. Lower-level pairs should be able to make a difference in the horse's stride without taking 100 strides to get there. If your horse is fighting you a bit, it is better to work it out in warm-up than wait until you have a jump in front of you! And this goes not just for the coming-back aids, it is equally important that your horse moves well off your leg.

Once you are ready to start jumping, pick one of the oxers (Jump A or D) and stay on a 20- to

30-meter circle. You can start with simple poles on the ground or a cross-rail, or when you're more experienced, start over a low square oxer.

While on the circle, play with your canters, alternating between collecting your canter and then opening it up. The key is to be able to approach a jump and be able to wait or go forward, depending on the canter you're schooling.

After you're warmed up and easily popping over the warm-up oxers, you can decide which line to start with. For the lazier lower-level horse or the more experienced upper-level horse, I would recommend starting with Line 1, measuring 72 feet. For the quicker lower-level horse or a greener horse, I would start with Line 2, measuring 66 feet.

Regardless of which exercise you start with, always set the jumps to a little below your competition height. Once you have successfully negotiated the exercise a few times, raise the jumps up to your competition height.

For this purpose, let's assume you are working with the quieter horse and start with Line 1. You are looking to have that more open canter that you practiced in warm-up. You want to have a little lighter seat, while being careful to not lean forward. This lighter seat simply allows your horse to canter on a bit more of a freer stride. You are looking to be able to get five even strides. This is very important, as it is counterproductive to get the five strides because of a sharp correction in the middle of the line. Even striding comes from establishing a good, steady rhythm on your approach to the vertical (Jump C) and then keeping that rhythm to the oxer (Jump A). Once you can do this, move on to Line 2.

Line 2 is 6 feet shorter than a standard five-stride line at 66 feet, so go back to your collected canter that you practiced in warm-up. Sit a little closer to the saddle so you are able to influence your horse a bit more, and remember to stay taller than you think you need to be. Even though this line is shorter than the first, you are still looking to accomplish it in five even strides. Again, establish the appropriate canter well before the vertical, and you should be able to accomplish this easily.

If you are on a speedier-type horse, start your jump school by trotting the vertical (Jump B) of Line 2, then concentrate on keeping a soft rein to the oxer (Jump D). The shorter distance will often naturally influence the horse to stay quiet between the fences. If the horse is insistent on rushing, you can carry this idea over to Line 1 by trotting into the vertical, landing in a quiet canter then coming back to the trot for the oxer. Depending on how persistent the horse

THE EXERCISES

is about rushing, you may spend an entire jump school just repeating these exercises. Then you can come back the next day and try to move on to a bending line, as illustrated by Line 3 (Jumps C and D) and Line 4 (Jumps A and B).

When you have successfully negotiated both exercises and shown the proper amount of adjustability, try some mini courses. There are endless possibilities, but to start I will often have my students start with Jump C straight ahead to Jump A, then collect while cantering left to Jump D straight ahead to Jump B. Then they will continue to the right to Jump C, and bend left to Jump D. Finally, they will continue to the right to Jump A, and bend left to Jump B. In an ideal world the bending lines would also be five strides, but this obviously depends on your arena and how you are able to set the exercise up. At all times, jump the middle of each jump—especially with a less experienced horse and rider, you should not angle the jumps at all.

When you start these mini courses, you can lower the jumps back down for the first time or two through. Bending lines can be quite difficult, so you want the jumps to be at a height where you and your horse are not worried. And remember that when you are starting the mini courses it's not going to be perfect the first time through. Bending lines require a lot of practice to get the right feel for them. So never get frustrated if it's not perfect from the beginning.

A horse's stride tends to shorten when in a turn. So while you are looking to carry your collected canter throughout the exercise, you want to feel like you are coming out of the turns and moving your horse forward to the jump. This is an exercise about learning feel, so I encourage my students to keep a positive attitude, as it will undoubtedly get better each time through.

When I'm teaching a more experienced pair—Preliminary or above—I challenge them with some harder modifications to the courses. I have them start going forward from Jump A to Jump C, then collecting for Jump D to Jump B. From there, they keep this collected canter and turn back to Jump C to Jump A, but I expect them to do it in six strides. Remember, this makes the exercise another 6 feet shorter, relative to the distance. So you really need to have your horse on your aids and listening to you. From here the rider can play a little with the bending lines of choice, and finally end with doing a direct line from Jump C to Jump D, and then a direct line from Jump A to Jump B. ◆

EXERCISE

Coursework

EXPERT

Sloane Coles

of Spring Ledge in The Plains, Virginia

This is a good exercise if you have a variety of horses to ride or train and want to set up something that can be utilized by everyone. The setup of this exercise also allows for plenty of room in the arena for flatwork, making it something you can leave set up throughout the week.

/ MATERIALS NEEDED

- 10 jump poles
- 10 sets of standards

/ SETUP

- Place the outside lines (Jumps D, E, F, and G) first.

- Then place the single fences, being sure that there are clear paths to and from each.

▽ **About the expert:**

A lifelong horsewoman, Sloane Coles is based out of her family's Spring Ledge in The Plains, Virginia. She has enjoyed a successful junior career, winning equitation, hunter, and show jumping titles at the country's top horse shows. As a professional, she has claimed victories at the Hampton Classic, HITS Saugerties, HITS Culpeper, and the Great Lakes Equestrian Festival. She made her Nation's Cup debut with Chippendale's Boy DZ at Calgary in 2019. ◆

www.springledgeva.com

35 /

/ WHY

This is one of those exercises you can often find set up in my arena at home. It is a versatile exercise that works for horses and riders of all levels so I can incorporate it into my jump schools and lessons regardless of the horse I'm sitting on or the rider I'm teaching.

You can also adjust the distances based on the size arena you have and the materials available to you. And depending on your level or goal for the day, you can do this with everything from poles on the ground to cavalletti to crossrails to 3-foot fences and higher.

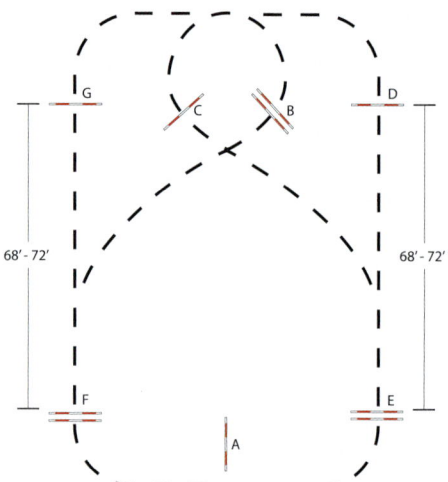

/ HOW

After you've warmed up on the flat, start over the simple vertical (Jump A)—or ground pole or cavalletti—on the short side of the arena. Your only goal to start is to make a perfect circle that goes through the center of your jump.

As you concentrate on this perfect circle, think to yourself, "Is my horse even and level? Is my horse landing on the correct lead every time, or is he favoring one lead over the other?" And instead of obsessing over fixing every imperfection, concentrate instead of your circle and riding your horse straight between your aids. Repeat until your horse is straight.

For horses more dominant on one lead over the other, concentrate on putting them into your outside rein, which in turn will help open up their inside shoulder allowing them to land on the correct lead. Patience is key!

GRID PRO QUO / *Margaret Rizzo McKelvy* /

From here, move on to Jumps B and C set on the diagonal. This simple pattern lets you practice both a long, straight approach to a jump and a shorter approach off a turn. Either way, you want to carry over the straightness you worked on with the first exercise into this exercise. The key to success is having your horse properly in your outside rein so that he doesn't fall in on the turns.

If you have a horse that doesn't have his lead changes yet, this is a great exercise to help teach them. When your horse lands on the incorrect lead, halt in a straight line, pushing him into your outside rein as you do so. By doing this you are setting him up for a lead change.

Now you're ready to ride your outside lines (Jumps D, E, F, and G). I prefer to set up a five-stride line, but again, you can play with this depending on the area that you have.

The goal here is to do five strides that do not change in length or rhythm. If this is easily accomplished, you can increase the challenge by adding strides and alternating between five, six, and even seven strides, meaning that your horse will need to compress and extend his stride within the same measured distance. But the most important thing is to keep the challenge appropriate for your horse.

Now you're ready to put all the pieces together. Again, create courses that are appropriate for your level, but also get creative. If bending lines are new for you, such as bending between Jump B and F or between Jump E and C, then leave those jumps as ground poles so you can practice without unnecessarily pounding on your horse's legs. And don't feel like you need to get everything done in one day. Work up to it over a week or month, but have fun with it while you do. ◆

EXPERT EXERCISE

Robert Costello

of Tanglewood Farm in Southern Pines, North Carolina

Traditional Gymnastic

▽ **About the expert:**

Based at Tanglewood Farm in Southern Pines, North Carolina, Robert Costello offers a clear, systematic, and no-nonsense training approach for both horses and riders. He is a USEA ICP Certified Level IV instructor and represented the United States at the 2000 Sydney Olympic Games and the 2003 Pan American Games. In addition to an active riding and teaching schedule, Robert is also the Chairman of the USEF Eventing High Performance Committee. ◆

www.rocequestrian.com

This is a great option for people who want to practice a canter gymnastic. The cones are also great tools to help riders practice their straightness, as well as their approach to jumps.

/ MATERIALS NEEDED

- 1 ground pole (optional)
- 10 jump poles
- 6 sets of standards
- 4 cones

/ SETUP

- This exercise is best set up on the centerline of your jumping arena.

- Your entrance and exit cones should be set approximately 3 to 4 feet apart in width.

- If you would like this to be a trot gymnastic, shorten the distance between Jump A and B to 18 feet.

GRID PRO QUO / *Margaret Rizzo McKelvy* /

- Keep an extra ground pole on hand in case you need an extra landing rail after Jump E.

/ WHY

There comes a point in both a rider's and a horse's training when the cantering of grids should become part of the repertoire. Practicing the cantering of grids only makes sense as ultimately a grid is a combination, and we don't trot combinations in competition. How often do we see a rider executing a lovely show jumping round only to have it all come apart at the first combination? This none-too-rare occurrence I see play out time and again as I travel about giving clinics as well as at the lessons I teach at home. We need to condition ourselves that riding into a combination simply requires us riding in good rhythm and balance on a straight line to a single jump. When we can achieve that, we've done our job. The rest is up to the horse. Of course, this is easier said than done, so like anything else, it demands practice (practice, practice). Just think of the cantering part of this exercise as an added benefit to what a well-designed grid should accomplish.

For the horse, this grid will test—and ultimately improve—straightness, balance, control, agility, rideability, and form over fences.

For the rider, this grid will test—and ultimately improve—control, concentration, position, effective use of aids, and plan execution.

The slightly shorter distances will encourage your horse to jump "around" the fences, creating the desired bascule in the air (as opposed to "at" the fences, which results in a flat, often careless jump). However, this is not a one-size-fits-all exercise and can be modified to suit your particular horse, as long as it stays appropriately challenging.

This grid is more on the advanced side but should be well within the capabilities for horses and riders schooling 2-foot-6-inch courses and above. It is a grid I've played around with and developed over a period of time. Those who have ridden in clinics with me will recognize at least parts of this exercise.

Note: *for greener horses and riders, the grid can initially be approached in trot. Simply shorten the distance between the first two elements to 17 to 18 feet.*

PRO TIPS

1. Grids are an opportune time to practice perfect position. The makeup of this grid should do a lot of the work for you, therefore, be thinking: Weight in the heel! Quiet upper body! Flat back! Chin up! Stable and consistent release in the air! Overall, there should be very little movement on your part in the air. Let your horse do the jumping.

2. Practicing grids without being fairly obsessed with straightness will dramatically reduce the positive effect the exercise is meant to have. Challenge yourself and your horse to approach, take flight, cruise through the air, land, and depart from the grid on the same line. Imagine as you complete your turn through the first set of cones that a train track has been laid down right through the middle of the grid and that your aids—legs, rein (opening, leading or guiding), eyes—are what keep it all on the rails! Your horse will never truly maximize his jumping potential if he is not straight.

/ HOW

To execute this exercise you need a ground person to help set jumps.

Set up cones at least four to five strides (48 to 60 feet) before the first set of standards, and at least five to six strides (60 to 72 feet) after the last set. As part of your warm-up, start by tracking left and practice trotting the pattern. Pay special attention to the quality of your turn through the first set of cones, the straightness of the trot through the empty standards, and finally the quality of your turn away from the exercise (light off the inside leg, connected to the outside rein, not leaning in nor bulging out) and subsequent 15-meter circle around the cone. Proceed down the long side of the arena and repeat the exercise a few times, alternating the direction each time.

> **Note:** *The use of the cones and the 15-meter circles are to aid the rider in executing a quality turn, a perfectly straight approach to and exit from the grid, and finally a well-balanced, rider-initiated turn after the exercise. This is a great exercise for horses that tend to "cut" the turn, or the riders who let them.*

Practice the same pattern in canter, starting on the left lead. This will be the same exact pattern you will use when the jumps are added. Track left and approach the cones from a left hand turn and continue absolutely straight through the empty standards. Well back from the second set of cones, transition to trot and

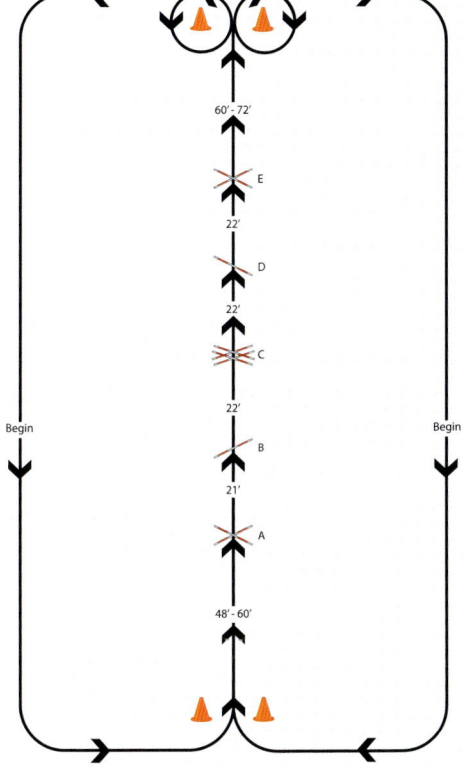

3. Do not be tempted to lengthen the distance in the exercise simply because your horse gets a little quick and finds it tight. Stick with your plan, stay soft, and let the jump do the "dirty work" for you. When he rubs a jump with no help from you he will come back the next time and take notice. If you ride the "hand brake" through the exercise and he still rubs a jump, most likely he will not have learned much. Just like humans, a horse will learn from his mistakes if allowed to do so on his own.

4. This exercise need not be completed in just one session. If you feel you need time just to conquer the pattern without the added pressure of jumps, come back to it the next time. Keep in mind that grid work should essentially be stress-free, as long as it is approached logically and systematically.

5. Above all else, keep it fun and enjoy the challenge this grid presents.

THE EXERCISES

establish the new right bend as you track right and canter on the 15-meter circle. Proceed down the long side of the arena and repeat exercise (tracking left the next time, and so on) until you can perform the pattern seamlessly and in balance.

Slowly add the jumps, starting at a height that you and your horse are comfortable with (preferably at least 2 feet 6 inches). As you feel your horse become more balanced through the turns, the 15-meter circle can be omitted though you will continue with alternating the direction as described above.

Note: *As you add jumps, the cones at the end of the arena will come up more quickly, requiring a quicker—though still smooth—response from you, the navigator.*

Jump A will be a simple tall cross-rail. It will look imposing (though in reality may only be 2 feet 6 inches in height in the middle) and have the effect of "holding" your horse's attention to the center of first jump. For Jumps B and D, the rail will purposely be set alternatively aslant. As is similar with Jump A, this will aid in keeping the horse straight. It is also a visual aid for you as the rider to keep your horse straight. If your horse tends to drift right, Jumps B and D will be three holes higher on the right, and vice-versa if your horse tends to drift left.

Note: *the height of the jumps should always be measured in the middle of the rail.*

Jump C will essentially be a Swedish oxer, and Jump E will be another tall cross-rail. A landing pole 11 feet after the final element can be used if your horse tends to land and quicken.

So as not to over-jump your horse, only jump the exercise once or twice before adding the next element or increasing the height. Keep all the jumps a similar height (taking the measurement in the center of the jumps), much like it would be in a combination in competition. The height of the exercise should be considered secondary to the aforementioned successful execution. ◆

EXERCISE EXPERT

Traditional Gymnastic

Sally Cousins

of Sally Cousins Eventing in Oxford, Pennsylvania, and Aiken, South Carolina

This is a great exercise for horses that tend to get a bit long and flat in their stride and need help regaining the balance needed for a show jumping course. This exercise also teaches riders to stay tall and strong in their position in tight distances.

▽ About the expert:

Based in Oxford, Pennsylvania, Sally Cousins has been a staple on the eventing circuit for more than 20 years. She has been the Leading Lady Rider of the Year six times and has competed at the world's premiere events, including Badminton, Burghley, and Kentucky. While Sally stays extremely busy competing, when she's not riding, she can be found teaching both at her farm and neighboring facilities. ◆

/ MATERIALS NEEDED

- 4 ground poles
- 3 cavalletti
- 3 jump poles
- 2 planks
- 5 sets of standards

/ SETUP

- This can be set up in almost any size arena and is best placed on the centerline.

- If your arena isn't long enough, the hogsback can be placed elsewhere in the arena.

www.sallycousins.com

THE EXERCISES

43 /

PRO TIPS

When teaching, I always tell my students not to bring the problems from their dressage work to the jump ring. If I have a horse that has trouble doing a rein-back or has trouble staying connected through a right lead canter depart, I might just let that go for the day. I don't want to start my jump school with a negative attitude, so I will instead concentrate on the flatwork exercises that my horse does really well and build from there.

- While planks are preferable, regular jump poles can be used. Each jump should have ground poles placed on either side as ground lines.

/ WHY

As equestrians, we all live for the thrill of galloping and jumping, and the same is true for most of our horses. But for eventers, in particular, the gallop—or canter, depending on your level—needed for cross-country is quite different than the canter needed in a show jumping round. When traveling at speed on cross-country, your horse can often get a little long and flat. And I find that after an event or a cross-country school, my horses are a bit more keen and sometimes a bit too eager than what is needed over a course in an arena.

This is my favorite jumping exercise for putting the technique back in a horse after a cross-country round. The tight 19 feet 6 inch distance between the two plank jumps is a great exercise to put the sharpness, carefulness, and roundness back into your horse's jump.

The cavalletti are great for teaching horses to adjust themselves and keep their balance with little involvement from the rider. Just like most gymnastic exercises, the job of the rider is to do as little as possible and simply stay balanced over the horse. With that said, once a horse has passed a certain level of experience, I typically stop trotting grids and instead concentrate on canter exercises.

I think it's important that the rider and horse can create roundness on their own. When I speak of "roundness," I am referring to the horse's trajectory over the jump. My goal for my horses as I move them up the levels is to shorten and heighten the trajectory over the jump. (I, of course, also want my horse to be round and connected between his fences, but this is not the roundness that I'm referring to in this case.)

GRID PRO QUO / *Margaret Rizzo McKelvy* /

If possible, I prefer to use planks instead of traditional rails for this exercise, as they are heavier and tend to make horses a little more careful.

While this is a very hard exercise, it is very appropriate for Novice-Level pairs. The placing poles are perfect for teaching a horse and rider how to see a distance. In a clinic with Hans Winkler that I rode in about 20 years ago, I learned that using placement poles is one of the best things you can do for your horse, and I have integrated them into my jumping exercises ever since. This particular exercise has evolved over time, and now I have it set up in my ring nearly all the time.

/ HOW

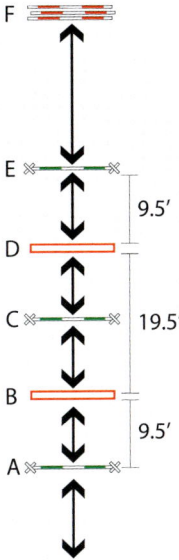

While warming up for a jump school, always practice creating and keeping the canters that you're going to need over fences. Depending on your horse's age, fitness, and competition level, your canter is going to be different. The canter that my green Novice horse needs is quite different than the canter my experienced Advanced horse needs.

Regardless of the canter, I do a lot of transitions, both from gait to gait (trot to canter, canter to trot, walk to canter) and within the gait. Not only does this help with your horse's adjustability, it also helps to keep your horse sharp off your leg.

For the Novice-Level horses, start by jumping Jump B with Cavalletti A and C set 8 to 9 feet out on both sides. In addition to the cavalletti, I also use ground poles on both sides of the plank rolled out a bit (typically to the edge of the standards). This indicates to the horse where his feet need to be on approach and takeoff.

As part of your warm-up, raise Jump B two holes at a time until it is at the rider's competition level. While warming up over Jump B, be very strict with yourself regarding your straightness. If you have striped jumps to use, focus on the middle stripe as you approach the fence. One good exercise to test your straightness is to halt a few strides after the fence, and then look back to your fence. Often, you will be surprised at how much you have drifted. If this is the case, no big deal, just practice some more!

If you have a horse that has a hard drift, there are a few things you can do to help yourself. One option is to put more poles on the ground in a chute before and after the fences to help keep your horse straight. Or, put a guide pole up to help keep him straight. With that said though, a horse that is drifting is usually looking to make more room for himself so he doesn't have to use himself. This tells me that there is probably a strength problem. So I will keep the fences low in the jump school and address the strength issue outside of the arena.

After you're comfortably and confidently jumping the warm-up Jump B in a straight line, lower this back down to a few holes below your competition height.

Add Jump D and Cavalletti E to complete your one-stride combination. Again, Cavalletti A, C and E—before, between, and after—and rolled-out ground poles will help dictate to your horse where he needs to be in terms of stride length and balance. As noted earlier, this 19 feet 6 inch distance is a bit tight, so you will probably need to come through a few times before your horse clues in to the tight distance. As the rider, your job is to sit up tall with your weight evenly distributed on both sides.

For more advanced horses, start their jump school with everything in place at a low height. To add a little bit of difficulty to the exercise, I like to raise the cavalletti around 6 inches off the ground. The raised cavalletti add a bit of height to the fence, so your verticals will never get much bigger than your competition height.

Once you're jumping the one-stride combination neatly and cleanly, you can add the hogsback (Jump F). While it would be great to set your hogsback up on a related distance to the centerline gymnastic, if your ring is not big enough, you can put your hogsback almost anywhere.

The hogsback gets horses to jump big and round, just as if they would over a cross-country rolltop or big oxer on course. By jumping the hogsback directly to planks, you are practicing what you have to do in competition, whether you're coming off a long, open gallop to a small jump on a Novice course, or jumping a maxed-out table to a combination at the upper levels. The toughness of this exercise comes from the rider having to change the canter from the open canter needed for the hogsback to the compressed canter needed for the combination.

As you can probably guess, this is a great exercise for horses that tend to rush. Typically, after a few hard rubs on the planks, horses will learn to slow down and pay attention. However, if the horse is intent on rushing, I lower the planks by a few holes so that they don't make a huge mess of it and scare themselves.

Once horses get used to the exercise, they learn to adjust themselves. I really believe in this exercise and do it almost weekly with my horses, and I tend to work it into most of my jump schools. While there are those super-careful horses that don't need an exercise like this, it is great for horses that need to be brought back after a cross-country school or gallop. ◆

GRID PRO QUO / Margaret Rizzo McKelvy /

EXERCISE EXPERT

Coursework and Traditional Gymnastic

Phyllis Dawson

of Windchase Farm in Purcellville, Virginia

These exercises are great for introducing more technical jumps in a friendly setting. Regardless of your discipline, being able to successfully navigate a skinny or corner jump will only make you a better rider.

▽ **About the expert:**

Phyllis Dawson competed at the highest levels of the sport for over 30 years and had success on many different horses, most of whom she trained herself. She represented the United States at the 1988 Olympic Games in Seoul on Albany II, finishing tenth Individually. Phyllis continues to concentrate on training and producing top-quality riders and horses at her Windchase Farm in Purcellville, Virginia. ◆

/ MATERIALS NEEDED

- 13 jump poles
- 2 skinny poles (optional)
- 12 sets of standards (or 11 sets of standards and 2 corner stands if available)
- 4 guide poles (optional)

/ SETUP

- These two exercises can be set up simultaneously on the quarterlines of your arena.

- If you don't have corner stands, you can use an extra standard or barrel or upside-down muck tub.

www.teamwindchase.com

THE EXERCISES

47 /

- Another option is to use skinny jumps instead of corners.

/ WHY

Eventing has evolved over the years, and the cross-country courses have become much more technical. Accuracy questions such as corners, skinnies, and angles have become increasingly difficult at the upper levels but have also become prevalent right down through the levels, with introductory accuracy questions being incorporated into Novice and even Beginner Novice courses.

Schooling methods have evolved as well, and we need to school our horses cross-country more than we might have in the past, with special focus on the accuracy questions. The rider must be able to hold the horse straight in the "corridor" between the two legs and the hands in order to teach the horse to hold his line and understand angles, narrows, and corners. At the upper levels, it must go a step further; the horses must learn to "seek the flags" and be looking for the next element, even when the face of the fence is less than 4 feet wide or set at an extreme angle.

Repetition of schooling these questions while gradually increasing the difficulty as horse and rider become proficient is the key to developing these skills. Although there is no substitute for getting out on the cross-country course, a lot of this schooling can be done in the arena by setting simulated cross-country questions with show jumps. I generally have my students jump some sort of accuracy exercise in every show jump school. I want these accuracy questions to become routine for both the horses and riders, so they become easy for them. One excellent way to do this is to incorporate them into grids—what better way to make corners and narrows become "no big deal" to both horses and riders? And for those who don't go south in the winter, it can be a fun way to break up the monotony when you are stuck in the indoor arena.

/ HOW

Before attempting to use these accuracy questions in gymnastics, you and your horse should be confident at the height you are schooling and able to comfortably jump through more straightforward gymnastic lines. You should also have a basic understanding of using the aids to hold the horse straight on the flat. But even for those with relatively little experience, these grids can be modified, with the help of guiding rails, to be appropriate for lower-level participants.

After you warm up, start with a single crossrail or small vertical (Jump A), and then add an oxer (Jump B) one stride away.

You can approach at either trot or canter. Greener horses and riders should generally start by trotting into the exercise, in which case I suggest the measured distance to be at 18 feet. More experienced pairings can canter in and use this as an opportunity to work on the quality of the jumping canter. If you decide to canter in, the space between Jump A and B should be lengthened to 20 feet.

GRID PRO QUO / *Margaret Rizzo McKelvy* /

Not only should you adjust the distances according to whether it is trot or canter, you should also take the stride length and level of the horse into consideration. Especially in the introductory phase, you want the gymnastic distances to be inviting and easy to help produce a confident and consistent jump.

When trotting in, start with a distance of 18 feet for one stride between Jumps A and B, and about 31 feet for two strides between Jumps B and C. When cantering in I would use 20 feet and 32 feet as a starting point. If the fences get set higher or the horses find the striding difficult, you can adjust these distances as needed.

After you are jumping this well, add another oxer (Jump D), set at a one stride distance.

Next is where it gets fun. Once you are doing the four fences (Jumps A, B, C, and D) easily, replace Jump C with a corner (Jump G). Make sure it is not too wide to start with, and keep the height easily within the horse's comfort zone. You can use a rail as a "wing" on the narrow end of the corner to assist in holding the horse straight.

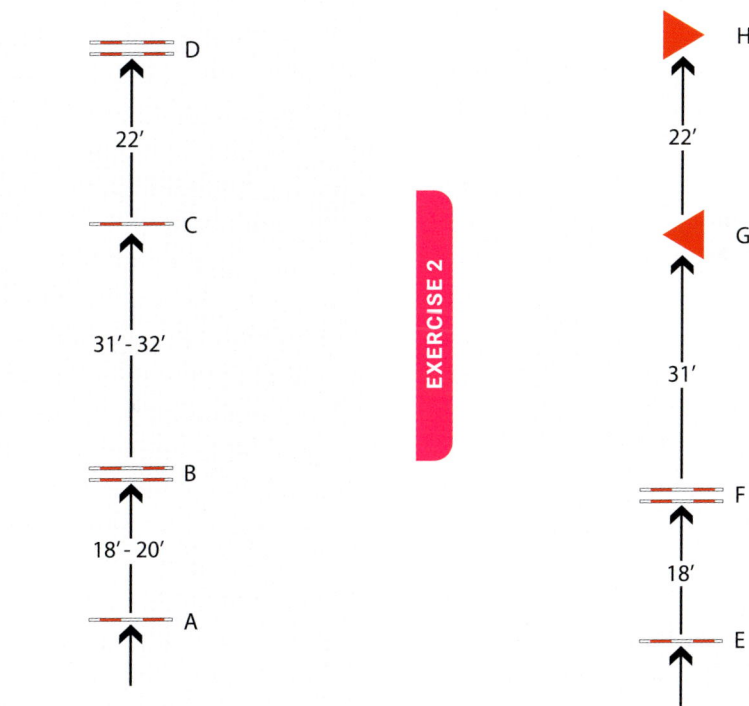

THE EXERCISES

If your horse negotiates it easily, you can gradually widen the corner to make it more challenging, being careful to keep the question appropriate for the level of the horse and rider.

Note: *With a higher-level combination where the corner gradually becomes quite wide, a barrel or jump standard can be positioned inside the wide end of the obstacle to make sure the horse does not try to jump into the middle of it.*

I like this as a method of introducing a corner to riders; I find many, when first asked to jump a corner, get overly aggressive and end up chasing their horses at it rather than keeping them organized and balanced. Introducing the corner in a gymnastic line prevents this from happening.

When you are jumping the gymnastic with the corner (Jump G) with ease, a second corner (Jump H) can be added approximately 22 feet (for one stride) after it. Again, guiding rails at the point help the horse understand how to hold his line. For horses and riders with more experience, the next step is to put the guiding rails on the ground, and then if he is jumping straight, to ultimately remove them altogether.

Another variation on this theme is to use narrow fences instead of corners. Again, guiding or balancing rails to help the horse stay straight should be used, then can be gradually removed for more experienced horse-and-rider pairs. There are endless possibilities; once the horse and rider are proficient, any gymnastic or grid you might build with regular jumps can be made with narrow fences instead. You can also incorporate corners and narrows into the same gymnastic line.

Throughout, the guiding principles should be to make sure both horse and rider are confident and competent over straightforward fences before introducing the accuracy elements. Use wings or guiding rails to ensure success. Adjust the difficulty of the question, the height of the fences, and the distances according to what the individual horse needs. Be sure to use these gymnastics in a way to show the horse and rider what they *can* do, not what they *can't*. Following these guidelines, you can use grids to practice cross-country questions such as corners and narrows until they become no big deal! ◆

EXERCISE EXPERT

Groundwork

Martin Douzant

of The Frame Sport Horses in The Plains, Virginia

Every good horseman knows that success starts from the ground up. Free jumping can be useful for horses of all levels, and when done properly, can have a real positive impact on their understanding of their jobs.

/ MATERIALS NEEDED

- 3 ground poles
- 5 jump poles
- 4 sets of standards
- Additional jump sets or gate panels

/ SETUP

- Ideally, this should be set up in an oval arena approximately 60 feet by 118 feet.
- If you only have a big area, simply use jumps or gate panels to make the space smaller.

▽ **About the expert:**

A native of France, Martin has dedicated his life to horses. The European systems of training are foundational to how he teaches riding theory, improves balance, and develops judgment in riders. He uses interesting and engaging exercises both on and off the horse to develop confidence, balance, and comprehension of the horse's movements. Martin offers lessons for every stage of competition. He loves to see others succeed and strives to support his students in their goals. ◆

www.theframesporthorses.com

- Use additional jumps or gate panels to round off your corners, which will keep horses from getting "stuck" in the corners.

- When setting up your chute, you will need several extra jumps or gate panels to make a "wall" next to your line of jumps. But be sure to leave a small space next to each jump to make it easy to walk through to adjust jumps.

/ WHY

Free jumping your horse through a jump chute is, in my opinion, the best way to assess the potential of a horse at a young age. Often, riders wait until a horse is already going under saddle to assess his jumping abilities, but by this time, you've already invested years into the horse. I've found that when done correctly and under the watchful eye of a seasoned professional, you're able to judge a young horse's potential as early as two years of age (but, of course, you need to keep it easy for horses that young).

Just as gymnastics are a super way to help a rider work on her own position, free jumping is a great way to help a horse with his jumping style, as well as to observe how your horse uses himself naturally. You get to watch him in his natural style, then decide how you'd like to improve him, and more importantly, how you can ride him better. For example, some horses jump with their heads low as they lift their withers, while others like to naturally keep their heads high. In either case, you would be able to adapt your own riding to better suit your horse.

Sending a horse through a jump chute is also an opportunity to see how your horse reacts to certain things, and to observe his natural instincts and his overall character over fences. While I often use free jumping with young horses, it's also a way to fix training problems you may have with an older horse.

As you get more experienced with free jumping, you will learn how to adjust the exercise to best suit your horse. But it's always a good idea to seek the help of someone experienced with running a jump chute as there is so much more to this than just chasing your horse over jumps. I only recommend skilled horse people do this.

/ HOW

Before you get started, you need to decide if you're going to do a "Catch and Release" method or a "Completely Loose" method. I'll explain the difference between the two:

Catch and Release: This is a more controlled environment, which is why it's mostly used at shows. You have the ability to control your horse's speed at entry into the chute. But this setup does require four people to execute it properly. You need one person to handle the horse at the entrance of the chute for the release, then one person to push the horse at the turn to the first jump, another person with a longe whip near your second two jumps, and then a final person to catch the horse at the end.

Completely Loose: This is a less controlled environment, but in my opinion, horses learn more in this setup. In this scenario, you have less control over how fast your horse goes, but I find this helps a horse learn from his own mistakes. Ninety-five percent of horses are fine with this setup, but there are still five percent that might not have enough groundwork experience to be able to respond to the positioning of the handlers, so these horses will need to do the Catch and Release setup. You need a minimum of two people for this, and your arena can be more open. Two people will be at the first turn and by your second two jumps. Depending on the size of your area, you will then need a few more people to help keep the horse going from the finish back to the start. You do need to have

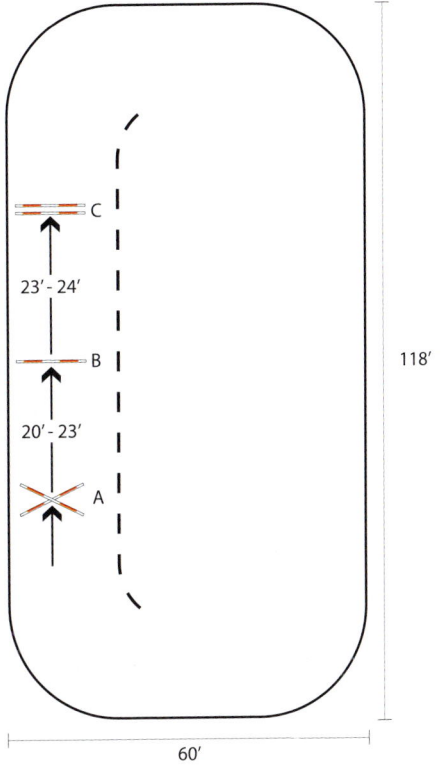

THE EXERCISES

solid fencing to ensure your horse doesn't jump out! Make sure all are prepared with comfortable barn shoes you can run in, as well as helmets.

Most competitions require three jumps: two small jumps to set the horse up for a final jump where he can express himself. However, it is possible to get a good result using only two jumps.

Once you are ready, start with all your jump poles on the ground. Hand-walk your horse once or twice through the chute, and trot him in hand once.

At this stage, your handler can release your horse at the beginning of the chute if you are using the Catch and Release method. You either catch him at the end, or he remains loose if you are using the Completely Loose method.

Once your horse is comfortable going through the chute on his own with everything on the ground, create your jumps. If you want to use fillers, such as flower boxes, in your jump chute, be sure to start off with them. I don't like changing the look of the jumps once the horse has gone through the chute.

First, create your first cross-rail (Jump A), then your second cross-rail (Jump B). From here, add in a final jump (Jump C), which will start as a vertical before changing to an ascending oxer. The next step is to change Jump B to a vertical, before gradually raising each jump. In total, your horse will go through the jump chute 8 to 12 times.

The height of the jumps is determined by how comfortable and confident your horse is. You don't want to raise things too quickly and risk scaring him. So be strategic in how you build your jump chute.

If you have a horse consistently going too fast, add a placing rail between Jumps A and B. Or, try raising the height of Jump B to get his attention.

On the flip side, if your horse is a little slow or timid, just take things slowly and help him realize that this is a "jumping game." ◆

GRID PRO QUO / Margaret Rizzo McKelvy /

EXERCISE

Coursework and Turning

EXPERT

Phillip Dutton

of True Prospect Farm in West Grove, Pennsylvania

Regardless of your discipline it is useful to be able to navigate a jump confidently and competently off a turn. This exercise is set up in a way that riders and horses of all levels can utilize and find benefit from it.

▽ About the expert:

Phillip Dutton is an international eventing athlete and seven-time Olympian with two team gold medals and one individual bronze medal. He has also twice represented the United States at the Pan American Games, winning two team gold medals and one individual silver medal. He has been the leading US rider 13 times and won the USEF Kentucky National CCI5* Championship four times. ◆

/ MATERIALS NEEDED

- 6 jump poles
- 5½ sets (11) of standards (or 5 sets of standards and 1 corner stand)

/ SETUP

- This is an easy exercise to set up, requiring just a few jumps, and it can go in your arena or field.

- If you don't have corner stands, you can use an extra standard, barrel, or upside-down muck tub.

www.phillipdutton.com

THE EXERCISES

55 /

/ WHY

While I have a variety of exercises I use to help teach my horses and students how to ride to a jump off a turn, this is one of my favorite exercises for teaching how to ride forward through a turn, while also being able to hold the line to the fences. In this day and age there are so many narrow fences and corners on our cross-country courses that you need to be incredibly accurate to make it through a course cleanly. The corner jump in the middle of this exercise will help you school these accuracy questions, and you can adjust the height and width of the corner depending on your level.

Another trend in modern course design is to see big tables off a turn, and the oxers in this exercise are great for learning how to deal with that question.

I try to stress to my students the importance of being adaptable on course, while still having a plan for each jump. This is a great exercise to practice this concept because there are so many striding options within the three jumps.

While schooling at home, I insist my students are able to do the three jumps in whatever striding we decide prior to them starting the exercise. Whether we decide they will stay wide for five strides between each, or stay close for four strides, or have five strides between the first two jumps and four strides between the second and third jumps, or vice versa. The point of the exercise is to create confidence in riders so they can go into an exercise with a plan and stick to it while schooling at home.

This transfers into riding at shows because my riders now have the skill-set to be adjustable on course and create options for themselves at different fences. As we all know, nothing ever goes exactly to plan while out on course, so you need to be adaptable and your horse needs to be adjustable. Since my students have schooled so many variations of this exercise, they have a variety of tools needed to make a quick adjustment to suit any situation.

/ HOW

Regardless of your level of riding, you should accomplish a few simple things in your warm-up that demonstrate your horse understands your aids. First, make sure he will promptly go forward when you put your leg on. Then that he easily collects when you simply sit taller and half-halt with a light rein aid. Finally, be sure your horse can turn in either direction with little resistance and while staying straight between the aids, meaning he shouldn't be bowing his shoulder out one way or another.

When having trouble with any of these tasks, spend some time tuning up your horse on the flat before moving on to jumping. The last thing you want is your horse to be surprised by a certain request in the middle of a jumping exercise. All of the going, "whoa-ing," and turning aids need to be cemented while in the flat warm-up.

When jumping, start in trot or canter depending on your level. But your first pattern will be to jump one of the oxers on the ends and do a sweeping rollback turn to the oxer at the other end, which will allow for you to work on your rhythm and straightness down the long side. Your pattern may change depending on the space you have to work with, but the goal is to show your horse both oxers from both directions.

Once your horse is doing this smoothly and without changing his rhythm, introduce the middle corner jump. Jump the corner from a long, straight approach, then turn to one of the oxers; repeat in the opposite direction. Do this a few times before stringing the entire exercise together.

As already mentioned, the beauty of this exercise is the number of options available with just three jumps. The distances are set so depending on which line you take, you have four or five strides between the oxers and the corner in the center. Start by consistently getting the same four or five strides—whichever is more appropriate for your horse—a few times before changing things up. Once you can reliably get

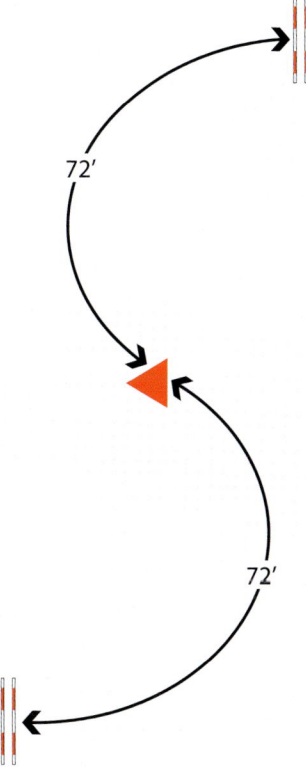

THE EXERCISES

those four or five strides between each set of jumps, challenge yourself by aiming for four strides between the first oxer and the corner, then five strides between the corner and the second oxer.

Regardless of the line you're riding, it's important to have a strong canter so that you meet the corner on a bit of a holding stride, with your horse then powering off the ground over it. While on course, you want your horse to be committed to the narrow type of fences, and this is the perfect way to school that feeling.

The most common issue I see while at shows is that horses are resistant on the landing side of the jump, and when given the chance most don't want to stay out on the turns. So, during this exercise you should work to make sure your horse is respectful of your inside leg.

While a corner may be intimidating to the lower-level rider, when constructed accordingly it is very appropriate for all level pairings. When you're still too intimidated by the idea of jumping a corner, start this exercise with a skinny jump in place of the corner; once you've mastered it, try the exercise with a corner in the middle.

The same goes for the oxers in terms of height. When starting this exercise, the jumps should be at your comfort level, but as you progress, don't be afraid to raise the height to your competition level at minimum or a little above to challenge yourself. ◆

EXERCISE

Traditional Gymnastic

EXPERT

Will Faudree

of Gavilan Farm in Southern Pines, North Carolina

This exercise helps riders learn to ride from their leg to hand, while helping horses learn to become more responsible for their own bodies. As is the case with many traditional gymnastics, the repetitive nature of this one allows riders to concentrate on their own position.

/ MATERIALS NEEDED

- 3 ground poles (optional)
- 8 jump poles
- 8 sets of standards
- 2 flower boxes (optional)

/ SETUP

- Neither of these exercises require a large space, but they should be set in a place where you can approach them from either direction.

▽ **About the expert:**

Based at his own Gavilan Farm in Southern Pines, North Carolina, Will Faudree quickly established himself as an accomplished international eventer. He has represented the United States in both the 2003 Pan American Games and the 2006 World Equestrian Games. He has competed internationally for over a decade and was a member of the silver medal Nations Cup Team at the 2010 Boekelo CCI4*. ◆

www.willfaudreeeventing.com

- If needed, get creative in their placement by putting them on diagonal lines in your schooling area.

- After your jumps are set, place your jump poles on the ground to start.

/ WHY

As equestrians, we are always looking to teach our horses to think on their feet and have that "fifth" leg that allows them to be responsible over fences. Gridwork exercises are great tools for sharpening up your horse's reactions, as well as helping you learn to stay balanced over fences. For eventers in particular, the reality is that we're jumping solid obstacles 50 percent of our competitive careers, so it's imperative that when things get tricky, your horse has the ability to think for himself and get you both to the other side safely, and you have the ability to stay balanced and out of his way.

Good horses become great horses when they're able to take care of their riders while doing their jobs flawlessly at the same time. Good riders become great riders when they're able to allow their horses to do their jobs. If you go to any international competition, you'll see horses that love their jobs and riders playing a supporting role. When the riders have to "ride" too much, trouble is bound to happen.

The tight distances in Exercise 1 and the spreads in Exercise 2 really force the rider to have a soft rein while riding to the deep distance. When you stay quiet and steady and let your horse jump up to you, your horse will learn to think for himself.

I find these two exercises really help to instill the method of riding from leg to hand. More importantly, you should be riding evenly on both sides, meaning that you should be balanced in the middle of the saddle and not shifting off to one side or another and unintentionally using one aid stronger than another.

/ HOW

Your flat warm-up should focus on self-carriage, as your flatwork is the time to make sure your horse isn't running through your hand. To test your horse's self-carriage, simply soften your hand and see what happens. If your horse falls forward or starts to rush when you soften the reins, keep working on your balance in the flatwork. Move your horse from side to side, ask him to come rounder and then stretch forward, lengthen his stride and collect it. All these things force your horse to think for himself and be responsible for his own body. When he stays in balance, perfect! You're ready to start jumping.

Once your flat warm-up is complete, start working through Exercise 1 with just poles on the ground. This helps both of you to tune into the distances. Trot through it a time or two, then canter through a few more times putting one stride between each pole.

From here, put all the poles up to small verticals and jump only the first and fourth verticals independently to quickly warm up your jump muscles. Jump these at an angle if needed to get in and out of the line.

Once you jump these single fences a handful of times, come around directly to the entire line of all four verticals right away. Remember this is a footwork exercise, so what better way to force your horse to use his feet than by surprising him a little with the four small verticals in a row. You've already thoroughly warmed up your horse on the flat so he is carrying himself and not leaning against the bit. You've also

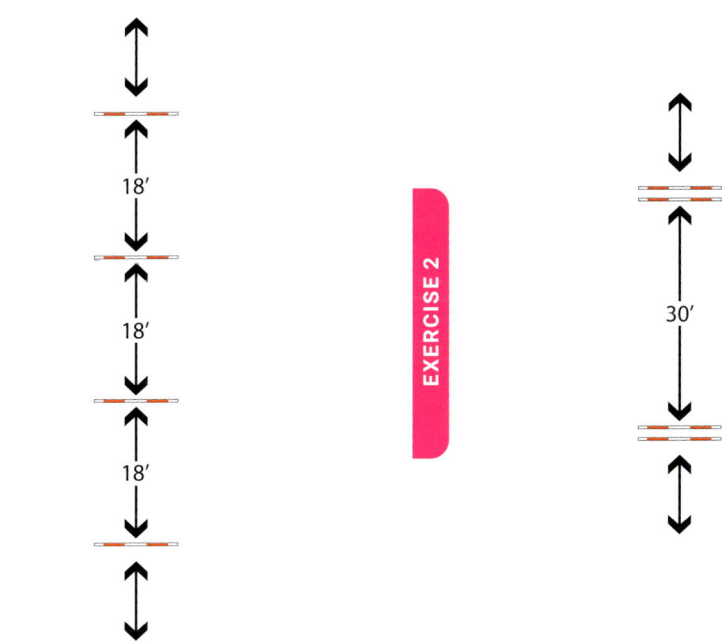

THE EXERCISES

PRO TIPS

When you're running into trouble with your horse rushing through the exercise, or even bouncing parts of Exercise 1, I put placement rails between all the verticals. This forces the horse to put a full step in and think about his feet. If your horse is still rushing, go back to your flatwork, and ask your horse to go forward and come back, and keep striving for that feeling that when you soften the rein, your horse stays in balance.

---

gone through the exercise with the poles on the ground. And by keeping the verticals small for the first few times through, you've done everything you can to set your horse up for success. However, if you're a greener rider or are on a greener horse, you can break the exercise down a little by starting off with just the first two verticals, leaving the third and fourth rails on the ground. This way the horse starts to understand the 18-foot distance before moving on to the full exercise.

The key to Exercise 1 is to ride with enough power in the canter to be able to answer the question of jumping competently through a series of tight distances. Don't mistake power for speed and lose your adjustability, which will catch up with you later.

This is the perfect exercise to teach a rider the difference between power and speed. I'll often ride up to the first vertical then make a conscious effort to soften my hand, which really gives my horse every chance to jump around the fences. You'll quickly realize that if you hold your horse to the first vertical, he will end up jumping too far in and run the risk of bouncing some of the distances.

As you work through this first exercise, don't worry about the height of the fences. I rarely make them bigger than 3 feet 3 inches, regardless of the experience level of the horse. The distance is tight enough (remember your typical one stride is 3 feet longer at 21 feet) so your horse is really going to have to rock back and power over the fences. If you were to make the fences too big, you would be making the exercise near impossible for your horse.

If you find your horse is skipping through this exercise without blinking an eye, raise the challenge without raising the physical expectations by alternating the sides that are raised on the vertical. The easiest way to accomplish this is to work through the exercise until you're at your desired height. Then lower one side two holes and raise

GRID PRO QUO / *Margaret Rizzo McKelvy* /

the opposite side two holes. When you look down the exercise, you should have alternating heights throughout.

After you've completed Exercise 1, give your horse a bit of a break so he can think about everything and let it settle. By this point, you should be amazed at how quickly your horse's feet are moving!

From here I move on to Exercise 2 and jump each oxer independently on an angle, just to give the horse a chance to see them. Then I approach the line of two oxers, putting two strides between the jumps, in the strong show jumping canter that Exercise 1 helped me create. You want to encourage your horse to jump in an almost slow-motion manner.

Once your horse is cantering through the exercise in a strong but connected canter, start widening the oxers. As the oxers get wider, your horse will start to really learn how to jump *across* something, so you need his canter to be quiet, connected, and thoughtful. You have two full strides before your next oxer, so there's no need to rush! For the more experienced combination, I actually widen the oxers *into* the exercise so that I make the distance a little tighter. For the more novice combination, I widen the oxers *out of* the exercise so that the middle distance remains unchanged.

As with Exercise 1, the height never gets above 3 feet 3 inches, regardless of a horse's experience, but I challenge the horses (and riders) by widening the oxers to up to 4 feet across. If you're worried about your horse stepping in between the rails, you can either put a rail diagonally across the top rails, put a brick wall or flower box in the middle so that the horse has something more solid to look at.

As the oxers get wider, and the distance gets smaller, use the same principles as you did in Exercise 1. Approach the fences with a strong, balanced canter that encourages your horse to jump from the base of the fence.

Keep in mind this is a tough exercise, so you won't master it immediately. Most gridwork exercises do all the work for you, whereas these two exercises are geared toward expecting your horse to keep his balance and self-carriage with minimal jumps. As a rider, your job is the same as it would be in a more traditional gridwork exercise, simply stay balanced and allow your horse to jump. Sometimes this is harder than being told to do four different things with your legs and hands. So be patient and let the exercise teach you. ◆

THE EXERCISES

EXPERT EXERCISE

Sandy Ferrell

of Royall Show Hunters in Hagerstown, Maryland, and Wellington, Florida

Cavalletti and Coursework

▽ **About the expert:**

A lifelong rider, Sandy Ferrell got her first pony at the age of four and never looked back. After a successful junior career, she graduated college with a degree in criminal justice and aspirations to work for the FBI. When the time came to choose between horses and a corporate career, Sandy chose the horses. She counts herself lucky to have worked with incredible horsepeople such as Louise Serio and Jack Stedding, before venturing out on her own to start Royall Show Hunters in 2002. Over the years, Sandy has produced numerous winning horses and riders, earning championships at all the major shows. ◆

These exercises are incredibly useful for helping riders smooth out their position without overtaxing their horses' legs. The average horse shouldn't jump more than once or twice a week, but the average rider needs to practice jumping skills more than that. These cavalletti setups are the perfect answer.

/ MATERIALS NEEDED

- 3 to 9 cavalletti

/ SETUP

- The distances demonstrated here are simply suggestions and can be adjusted to fit your space.

- You can either set these up all at once or adjust the placement and progress through the exercises.

- For an extra challenge, you can set the cavalletti in a field to utilize the terrain.

GRID PRO QUO / *Margaret Rizzo McKelvy* /

/ WHY

In all the roles I've had in my career, being an instructor is my favorite. It's what I love to do the most, and over the years I've learned that all you need is 6 to 8 cavalletti to teach someone to ride better or to get a horse better trained.

Success over fences is never about how high you can jump or if you can find the perfect distance every time to a jump, it's about these two things: 1) having complete body control, and 2) having a truly "broke" horse.

When I reference a "broke" horse, what I mean is, does your horse respond to your aids when you apply them. Does your horse go forward when you put your leg on? Does he stay neutral when you're quiet? Does he come back when you half-halt? And can you keep a constant connection with your horse throughout? Regardless of what you want your horse to do, your body dictates the quality of the connection as you ask him to tackle whatever task you put in front of him.

As a trainer, my top two priorities when working with students are developing and perfecting their body control, along with developing and perfecting their connection with their horse. Any successful partnership is a result of communication and compromise, and this is true for both horse and rider.

These particular exercises are my favorites because they focus on these two issues. Plus cavalletti aren't physically challenging for horses, so riders can really practice and repeat this exercise without worrying about unnecessarily pounding on their horse's legs. And I believe that if you can't do an exercise properly over cavalletti, you shouldn't be jumping any higher.

There are also plenty of variations that you can make with these cavalletti, depending on what you want to work on. You can set them up on a straight line, on a semi-circle, or even a serpentine, depending what you want to focus on. Regardless, these cavalletti are all about getting the rider to build a proper connection with the horse. It's constructive without being destructive.

/ HOW

Depending on the size of the space you have available to you, you can set your striding any way you like as far as the number of strides. The difficulty comes with how you want the strides to ride—short, long, or neutral—and how you combine them. My particular favorite is to do a short line to a long line (Cavalletti C to B to A), which then becomes a long line to a short line from

the opposite direction (Cavalletti A to B to C) as illustrated in Exercise 1.

Because your horse won't be giving you a big bascule over the cavalletti, there are a lot of options to work on your adjustability. The quiet four strides could become a forward three strides, or the long four strides could become a collected five or six strides. The possibilities are endless, and it's great to practice.

As you work your way into this exercise, always keep Cavalletti B as your priority. How you get to Cavalletti B will determine how you exit the exercise. And while it seems counterintuitive, you should almost look over Cavalletti A or C (depending on which direction you're going), and instead just view it as nothing more than a placing pole on the ground before Cavalletti B. There should be little to no releasing over the cavalletti, and your horse must shorten and lengthen his stride rather quickly.

Try to be very self-critical as you work through these cavalletti. Are you throwing your body up your horse's neck in the long part? Are you relying on your hands for the short part? If you're smart, you'll be able to pick out some of your own bad habits, or pick up on places where your horse is lacking. Then take a moment to think about what went wrong, how you can make it better, and try again. The distances between each cavalletti are short enough so you have to react quickly, and when you don't, the exercise will tattle on you and expose your weaknesses.

And if you make a mistake, don't worry! That's what makes this exercise so great because you can go about fixing it, and that's what

EXERCISE 2

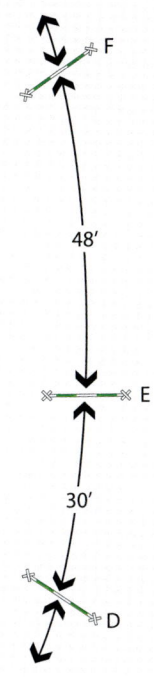

EXERCISE 3

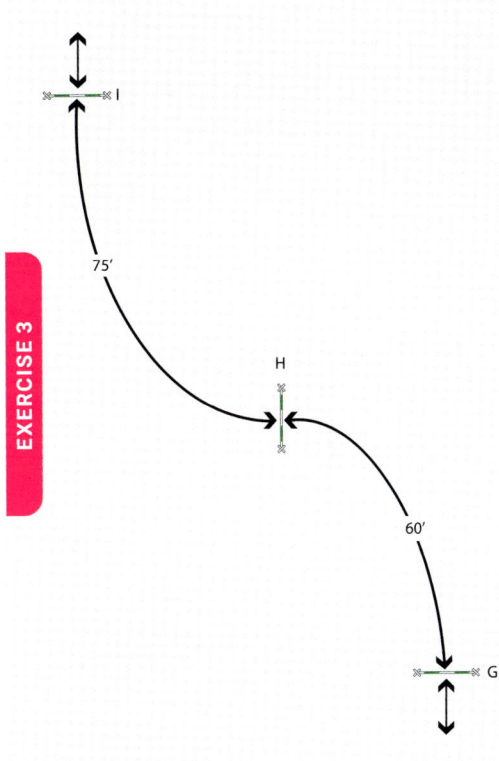

makes you a better rider. A common trouble spot often occurs when you have to ride in forward for the first part, and then collect for the second part. A lot of things can go wrong when you are late to collect or your horse's mouth is tough. This usually means that you've lost your horse's straightness, and we all know that when your horse isn't straight, it's impossible to adjust him correctly. Keeping your horse straight is both the hardest and most important job you have as a rider.

If you're struggling at all with this exercise, try holding your jumping whip horizontally over your horse's neck, holding the reins and whip at the same time. This will keep your hands in one position so you have to rely on your other aids—leg, voice, and most importantly, your core—to get things done. This also helps to open up your chest and shoulders, which allows your core to engage more easily.

As a result, the contact with your horse's mouth becomes much more consistent. And a more consistent contact enhances your communication and increases your chance of success. It may not be perfect, but this will help you improve.

Once you've conquered the straight line, change the cavalletti layout. Arranging the cavalletti in a semi-circle (Cavalletti D, E, and F) as illustrated in Exercise 2 or serpentine (Cavalletti G, H, and I) as illustrated in Exercise 3 presents some new challenges. But remember your approach to success will always be the same. Never deviate from straightness, body control, and communication. Also try to always talk to your horse and tell him what you'd like to accomplish while it's happening. Our horses are very in tune with our voices and they like hearing from us.

You know you're ready to wrap up your jump school for the day when you know exactly what you need to do to get your horse to collect and lengthen for all of your different striding, while remaining in a quiet connection.

If you made quick work of these three cavalletti, don't just put them away for the year. I like to leave this setup in my arenas to check in with from time to time. Sometimes that's at the beginning of a jump school. And other times, I will come back to this when I'm struggling with a course. This exercise tells you what you're lacking so you can go back and tackle your course with a better idea of what you need to work on.

When you go into the show ring, you want to look at the course and think that it is going to be a piece of cake. Everything you do at home should be more challenging than what you're doing away from home. So really utilize this exercise to help you in your coursework. Memorize the feeling of Cavalletti A to B in four, five, or six strides, or the feeling of Cavalletti B to C in three or four strides, and utilize that on course. And be sure to remember what level of intensity you need in order to create that feeling as it will help you succeed in the arena. ◆

EXERCISE EXPERT

Cavalletti

Peter Foley

of Woodhall Farm in Aldie, Virginia

This is a great exercise for those with limited space and materials. It's perfect for practicing footwork without overtaxing your horse's legs.

/ MATERIALS NEEDED

- 2 to 4 ground poles
- 5 to 10 cavalletti

/ SETUP

- This exercise doesn't require a lot of space, making it easy to set up in almost any size arena.

- You can either set both scenarios up at once or adjust the placement as you progress through the exercise.

- If you do not have cavalletti, you can use jumps and leave them quite small.

▽ **About the expert:**

Top hunter trainer Peter Foley trains out of his Woodhall Farm in Aldie, Virginia, with his business partner of 30 years, Dale Crittenberger. Their farm specializes in training horses, ponies, and riders in hunters, jumpers, and equitation, with winners from local shows to Devon. They've trained riders to multiple state equitation finals championships, as well as multiple national champions. ◆

THE EXERCISES

EXERCISE 1

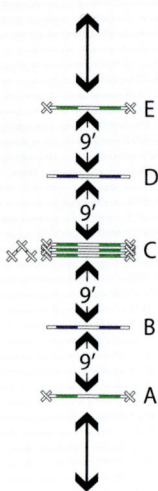

EXERCISE 2

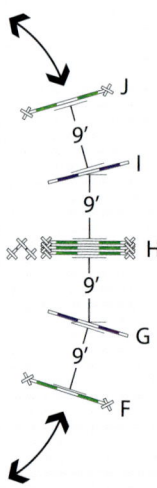

/ WHY

There are so many reasons to love this exercise, from the ease of setup to the wide range of horses and riders that it can be used for. You often find this setup in my arena, and it's something that I encourage my students to practice when not in lessons. I'll often incorporate it into coursework as well. The nice part about using cavalletti is that they provide fairly low-concussion exercises for your horse, so you can repeat them without worrying about pounding on your horse's legs.

While I use this exercise primarily for my hunter clients, there is a lot here to benefit horses and riders from all disciplines. For hunters, especially, it's not just about clearing the jump, it's about the shape of the jump. We strive to create a rhythm where the horse's steps before and after the jump are the same. A good hunter will start and finish on the same stride length, and this exercise helps to create that.

The other nice thing about this exercise is that your success isn't dependent on finding a perfect distance because the "jumps" are so small, especially at the start. The tripod of cavalletti (C and H) help create a better bascule over the jump, which benefits horses of all disciplines.

/ HOW

Start with just Cavalletti A, Ground Pole B, and just a single cavalletti for Cavalletti C to start. You will add in the additional cavalletti to create the tripod at C later. The 9-foot measurement is

GRID PRO QUO / Margaret Rizzo McKelvy /

an average distance that works for most horses. And for hunter horses, this is a distance they need to become comfortable and proficient with.

From here, you can add your Ground Pole D and Cavalletti E. And finally build up your cavalletti tripod.

Keep in mind there's nothing preventing you from stopping at any of these building points. Be honest with yourself about your and your horse's ability, and what you want to accomplish on any given day. However, if you've mastered the first setup (Exercise 1), move on to something a little more challenging by putting a slight curve into the exercise (Exercise 2). Typically, we want to see our riders give a crest release to allow the horse to use his head and neck. But in more modern derby and handy classes, we need the horse to follow the rider's hand.

By putting this exercise on a bit of a curve, you teach the horse to follow your hand in what is more of an automatic release. This really tests the communication between you and your horse. Does your horse resist when you use your hand? If so, work on this leg-to-hand connection on the flat, then approach the cavalletti again. Remember, it's not about manhandling your horse around a course but building a connection so you're able to seamlessly guide him.

For more advanced riders, you can up the challenge a bit more by adding flower boxes or other filler. My most advanced riders start with the exercise already built up this way, versus setting it up step by step.

Remember, the goal isn't to make your horse jump higher or harder, but for him to jump *better*. When you have a short-strided horse, you might inch out the distances a little to encourage him to lengthen, but a good hunter has a default stride, and this is your end goal. I like to keep my distances fairly standard because I never want my horse to feel like he is trapped. I want him to learn that if he finds his default canter, everything will be easy. ◆

THE EXERCISES

EXPERT EXERCISE

Traditional Gymnastic

Patty Foster

of Rolling Acres Show Stables in Brookeville, Maryland

About the expert:

After years of fox hunting and showing as a junior and amateur, Patty started Rolling Acres Show Stables in 1982. Patty has trained champions from small ponies and short stirrup divisions to amateur-owner and junior hunter titles. She has a unique talent of matching a horse with a rider and making them a successful, competitive team. Patty also manages the sales and leasing duties for the show stable. ◆

www.rollingacresshowstables.com

This is an easy-to-set-up exercise that doesn't take up a lot of room in your arena. It can be utilized for horses and riders of all levels and can also be incorporated into coursework.

/ MATERIALS NEEDED

- 2 ground poles
- 2 jump poles
- 2 sets of standards

/ SETUP

- This exercise can be set up most anywhere in your jumping arena or field.
- It is recommended to have a few extra ground poles on hand if needed.

GRID PRO QUO / *Margaret Rizzo McKelvy* /

/ WHY

This is one of those exercises that helps riders of all levels, whether they are prepping for their first show or for their first championship. The ground poles really make horses study the exercise, which, in turn, forces them to slow down and think their way through it. For the rider, this helps her get the feeling of her horse backing off on his own so she can concentrate on her own position and keeping her leg on.

While this exercise really works on the horse's style and form, which is imperative for hunter riders, I think that it crosses disciplines well, and anyone can benefit from it. Every sport horse needs the same set of canters to be successful. They all need to be able to collect and extend, and rock back on their hind end and use themselves. The basics are the basics regardless of your discipline.

I also love this exercise because it's so versatile, while also not taking up a lot of room, so you can leave it set up in your arena throughout the week and come back to it when you need it.

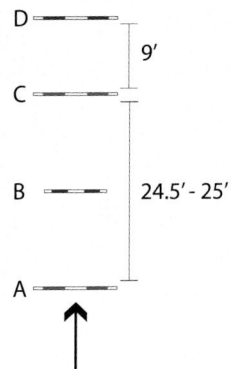

/ HOW

Whenever you warm up, you want to make sure you test all your "buttons." Ask your horse to lengthen his step and collect his step in a manner that is appropriate for his level of training. The end goal for your warm-up is that you're able to organize your horse effectively and efficiently.

Once you're ready to start jumping, start with just Jump A and let your horse warm up his jump muscles.

Then add a Ground Pole B 9 feet behind your warm-up vertical and jump through that a few times.

Then add in the rail of Jump C and roll out your Ground Pole B to be in the middle of the two jumps. If you're a more advanced rider, you're welcome to start your jump school here with two small verticals and a middle ground pole.

Once you're comfortable with this one-stride combination, add in Ground Pole D 9 feet from the back of your second jump.

As you work your way through this, keep trying to find that perfect quiet distance to Jump A. When you chase the horse to the jumps, this exercise will quickly teach you how to slow down so you can find that quiet, but powerful canter needed to successfully negotiate a course of fences.

When you're successfully navigating this line of jumps as is, the next step is to adjust the distances between Jump A and C a bit to play with your horse's stride length. And when you're a more advanced rider and want to challenge yourself, build up the jumps a bit to work on your horse's style over the fences. ◆

EXERCISE EXPERT

Traditional Gymnastic

Ariel Grald

of Ariel Grald Equestrian in Southern Pines, North Carolina

This is a great exercise for riders who have limited jumps to work with, and perhaps limited space. The setup is easy, and the distances are versatile for horses of varying abilities.

/ MATERIALS NEEDED

- 4 jump poles
- 4 set of jump standards
- Flower boxes or other filler (optional)
- Extra ground poles for warm-up

/ SETUP

- You can place this exercise most anywhere in your arena, as long as you can approach it from both directions.

- Place a few ground poles randomly around your arena for warm-up.

▽ About the expert:

Based at Annie Eldridge's Setters' Run Farm in Vass, North Carolina, Ariel Grald has competed through the five-star level on her long-time partner Leamore Master Plan. Ariel enjoys developing young horses through the top levels, as well as helping riders reach their goals. ◆

www.settersrunfarm.com

/ WHY

Throughout my everyday training, I try to keep a big focus on rider responsibility versus horse responsibility. To keep it very simple, the preparation for any jumping exercise—namely creating a good, balanced canter to jump from—is completely the rider's responsibility. Once you get on your line for the exercise, it's the rider's job to stay balanced in the middle and out of the horse's way, as the responsibility is transferred to the horse.

The purpose of this exercise is to combine footwork with coursework. The 21-foot, one-stride distance is your footwork piece, and the 45-foot, three-stride distance is your coursework piece. The challenge is maintaining three strides of even length to your last vertical, and for the horse to remain careful for the last vertical.

Regardless of the level you're competing, your horse is more likely to get flat and unbalanced the longer you have between fences. This is why practicing how to develop and maintain that perfect show jumping canter is so important. Three strides is the perfect distance to set yourself up for success.

/ HOW

Before you even jump the first jump, be sure your horse is sufficiently warmed up through his body. Try to start with a walk hack whenever possible, then ask him to lengthen and come back within each gait, along with some low-stress lateral work. While your expectations of the horse will change depending on his level of training, he needs to listen to all of your aids, regardless of whether you're flatting or jumping.

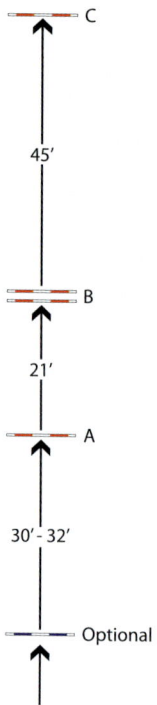

Once you're confident your horse is properly warmed up on the flat, start trotting and cantering over the ground poles that you have scattered around the arena. This is the time for you to help create the shape and balance to the canter that is appropriate for jumping. Remember, at all times, the horse needs to be responsible for his own feet.

From here, simply start with the whole line of jumps (Jumps A, B, and C) set quite low for your level of jumping. This setup is not intimidating, so for a horse that knows how to jump, it shouldn't be too difficult to start with all the

GRID PRO QUO / Margaret Rizzo McKelvy /

jumps in place. Of course, if you have a green horse, you can start with the poles on the ground and build it up jump by jump.

As you work through this line of three jumps, you want to keep a few things in mind before you raise the jumps. The biggest thing is to analyze your three-stride combination between Jumps B and C and make sure your horse is taking three even strides. If your horse is landing and rushing a little bit, add a landing pole after Jump B, and, perhaps, add another one in front of Jump C.

On the opposite end of the spectrum, when you have a horse that is a little lazy and behind your leg, add in a canter circle before Jump A. Practice going forward and collecting back on this circle, making sure you can go beyond your perfect canter and come back to a canter that's a little smaller than perfect, and finally settle in the middle on that perfect canter before heading to Jump A.

Another thing to consider is whether your horse is truly straight through the entire exercise, which includes the few strides before and after the entry and exit. If you have a horse or rider really struggling with straightness, add guide poles on the ground next to the jumps to help them out.

It's important to keep riding after Jump C, so give yourself something to ride toward. You can get creative with this, and it can be anything from a set of cones to ride through to a cavalletti set on a bending line. Remember your transition back down to the walk between jumping rounds is also part of your exercise. Make every transition count, rather than celebrating after the last vertical and letting your horse fall on his forehand or get crooked.

As you work through the exercise, there are two ways of making it more challenging. You can build up the jumps gradually until they are at your competition height. Or, you can make the jumps more visually interesting by adding or changing the fillers throughout your jump school. And for more advanced horses, use the distance to challenge them a bit by shortening the distances a little to teach them to compress and move their feet faster.

In addition, as a way to help work on finding that perfect distance while on course, you can add a ground pole two strides away from Jump A to help practice finding that distance. Just remember that the more poles you put on the ground, the more your horse has to think. I tend to either add poles or raise the jumps, but rarely both at the same time.

I often find that working through this exercise is enough for one jump school. But as your horse becomes more familiar with it, you can always use this as a warm-up as preparation for coursework. ◆

THE EXERCISES

EXPERT EXERCISE

Coursework and Traditional Gymnastic

Peter Gray

of Wentworth in Orangeville, Ontario

▽ **About the expert:**

Peter Gray has competed in three Olympic games, two World Equestrian Games, is a Pan American Games individual bronze medalist, and has competed at most of the prestigious international events in Europe, including Badminton, Burghley, Le Lion d'Angers, Saumur, Boekelo, Luhmühlen, and Punchestown, and Kentucky in the United States. In addition to his eventing, Peter has campaigned three different horses at FEI-level dressage, enabling him to compete at the Grand Prix level. He's also committed to giving back to the sport and serves on many international and national committees. ◆

This setup is great for combining a little gymnastic work with a little coursework. It also helps riders work on carrying their position from the gymnastic throughout an entire course.

/ MATERIALS NEEDED

- 7 ground poles
- 2 cavalletti
- 6 jump poles
- 1 gate
- 1 plank
- 7 sets of standards

/ SETUP

- This course requires a bit of space. If you don't have a large enough arena, break the parts up a little and get creative in your placement.

- If you do not have any heavy gates or planks available to you, you can utilize flower boxes

GRID PRO QUO / *Margaret Rizzo McKelvy* /

or other fillers with regular jump poles to make a jump appear more substantial.

/ WHY

I teach numerous clinics throughout the year, along with my regular teaching at my home farm, so I see a variety of horses and riders on a regular basis. Regardless of whether I'm teaching a high-performance rider or an amateur looking to get around her first schooling show, the emphasis is always the same: training the fundamentals of correct, confidence-building riding, as well as using every training session to work on the partnership with her horse.

Gymnastics are a good thing to practice throughout the year, as they train athletic ability over fences, creating a better bascule over the jump. In a simpler way, they are also good strength-building exercises, as they specifically work on the pushing ability from the hind end. Using gymnastic exercises, you are able to improve your skills related to shortening your horse's stride and getting to the base of the jumps. You can also work on your own position and on your lower-leg strength through a series of jumps.

/ HOW

While working through the three principals described in the sidebar on p. 80, take the time to walk and trot over some ground poles (Ground Poles G and H) to get the horse confident about his job ahead. Additionally, this gives the horse a chance to coordinate his legs for jumping,

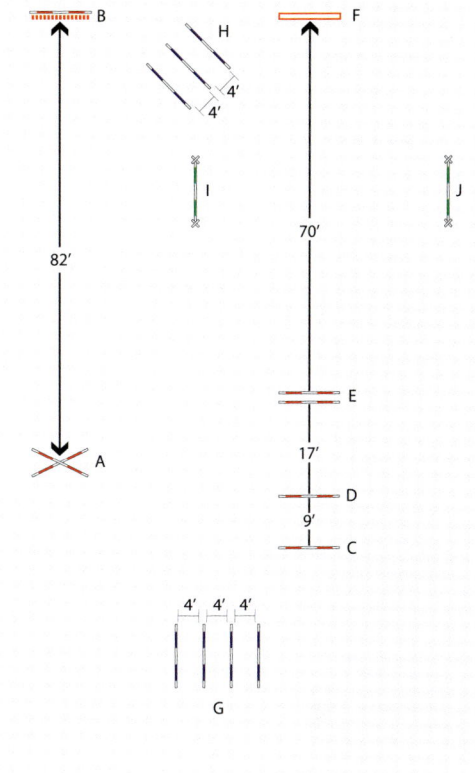

which is especially important for young horses. Before you head toward the first jump, create a simple cross-rail somewhere to warm up over, and continue to ask yourself these questions:

1. *Is my trot balanced?*

2. *Is my horse connected?*

3. *Do I have a tempo that doesn't change?*

THE EXERCISES

PRO TIPS

Before you begin the gymnastic exercises, I want to have a brief conversation about the warm-up. I'll never forget many years ago when one of my trainers suggested I might as well chase my horse around the paddock with a longe whip because my riding wasn't doing anything useful to prepare him for jumping. That really stuck with me, and I now always like to answer the following three questions before I move on to jumping in a schooling session:

1. Am I—and is my horse—relaxed?

2. Is my horse supple?

3. Is my horse responsive to the aids—forward from the leg and collecting from the half-halt?

Keep in mind that these same rules apply for warm-up before any type of competition!

4. *Do I have an appropriate amount of impulsion?*

5. *Is my line accurate?*

To help make sure you are "with the motion" for the jumping takeoff phase, create a half-seat position without posting at least 30 feet before the jump. Not only does this help with your balance, it's also a great lower-leg strengthening exercise.

Once you've answered all these questions on the flat and over the simple cross-rail, you're ready to tackle the first exercise. This exercise is very straightforward, because the point is not always to jump a lot of big fences, but to perform simple exercises well. And while I have a notebook of countless gymnastic exercises with increased difficulty, I think this first one is a great introduction to jumping for horses and riders of all levels.

To start you will trot Jump A, landing in the canter and continuing on to Jump B. As you're cantering toward the gate (Jump B), you should already be thinking about something useful to do after you land from Jump B. Depending on the level of your horse, this could be a flying change, a halt, leg-yield, or a simple circle.

Regardless, as you're working on your landing exercise, you should at some point come back to the trot and find your way back to Jump B. Now, trot Jump B and canter back to Jump A, again finishing the exercise with an appropriate balancing routine.

Repeat this pattern at least twice before raising both jumps 4 inches or so, and then repeating the pattern again, but over the bigger jumps. The focus of this exercise is not how big you can make the jumps, but *how good you can make the canter between* the jumps. And this may surprise people, but I don't always insist on the horse being on the correct lead between the two jumps. Instead, I think it's a great place to work on the counter-canter, plus there

GRID PRO QUO / Margaret Rizzo McKelvy /

really isn't enough time to prepare a young horse for a flying change. Instead, use this as an opportunity to create balance on either lead.

From here it's time to move on to the second part of the exercise, involving Jumps C, D, E, and F, a good introduction to a series of jumps in a row at a shortening distance, which is the definition of a "gymnastic."

You should trot into the bounce (Jumps C and D), as young horses are more confident trotting jumps, and most riders can always work on trotting jumps better.

If you have a young horse, you have the option of placing a ground pole halfway between Jump D and Jump E, which will help a young horse with the shortening aspect of jumping.

On landing from Jump E, you should canter away right into a fairly crisp transition to a halt before Jump F. But don't let this halt transition fool you into thinking that your canter should be weak. Quite the opposite is true—you should land off the oxer in a forward canter that is balanced, straight, and has an even tempo.

Once the horse has relaxed into this routine, you can progress to completing that same line by jumping Jump F. Ideally your halt routine has created an adjustable horse and made a half-halt available to you after Jump E.

Your next phase of the exercise involves Cavalletti I and J on the bending lines. The cavalletti should be raised about 2 feet off the ground, and you can get creative in the construction, using either standards or a pair of plastic blocks. To start, trot into the bounce (Jumps C and D) and create a little left flexion upon landing, which will encourage your horse to land on the left lead.

After Jump E, continue on to Cavalletti I. The goal is to reestablish a balanced canter before you finish your half-circle to the cavalletti. This will teach riders to focus on balancing the canter promptly on landing after fences and resist any urge to ride backward on the final approach to a jump.

After Cavalletti I, you again want to do something useful on the landing side, and if your horse is ready, this is a great opportunity to introduce the flying change (if your horse lands on the wrong lead). Repeat the exercise, but this time add right flexion after the bounce and continue on to Cavalletti J on the right side.

As you move through these exercises, keep asking yourself the same three questions from your warm-up (see sidebar). If at any point you can't answer "yes" to those questions, take a step back and reestablish the basics. ◆

THE EXERCISES

EXPERT EXERCISE

Traditional Gymnastic

Sam Griffiths

of Griffiths Eventing Team
in Gillingham, Dorset, England

About the expert:

An Australian native, Sam Griffiths has represented his home country at the 2010 World Equestrian Games and the 2012 and 2016 Olympic Games. In between his Olympic appearances he won the 2014 Badminton CCI5* with Paulank Brockagh. He believes that correct training is the foundation to success at every level in every discipline. He enjoys training horses and riders of all levels. ◆

www.samgriffithseventing.co.uk

This is the perfect exercise to help a horse work on his balance if his canter has been getting a bit flat and the rider needs help getting the canter sharp again. The distances are also easily adjustable, depending on what you need to accomplish that day with your particular horse.

/ MATERIALS NEEDED

- 2 to 3 ground poles
- 3 jump poles
- 3 sets of standards

/ SETUP

- If you are limited in space and materials, this is a good exercise to try.

- It is easiest to set up on your centerline so that you can alternate your approach.

GRID PRO QUO / Margaret Rizzo McKelvy /

/ WHY

This is one of those jumping exercises that any horse can do, whether you have a horse just starting out over fences or have an experienced FEI competitor. The distances can be easily adjusted to best suit your horse's experience level, making this a great exercise to have available in your arena.

This also makes a great exercise after a cross-country run as it helps get a horse's technique back after flattening out while galloping cross-country.

/ HOW

While warming up for this jumping exercise, make sure to test all your canters. This means doing a lot of transitions *within* the gaits, not just between the gaits. Your horse should easily and seamlessly adjust his stride length before you tackle your first jumps.

The reason you want to make sure all of your "buttons" work is because this is an exercise that involves a collected canter into the first placing pole (Ground Pole B). The collected canter takes away a lot of the speed, so the horse has to use his power and, more importantly, his technique to jump cleanly.

To start, set up your Ground Pole B, 9 feet to a small vertical (Jump C) with a placing pole 9 to 10 feet after. You should jump this setup a few times, then go ahead and raise Jump C to your competition height.

From here, add in the front pole of your oxer (Jump E). This allows the horse to learn the exercise before it becomes really tough.

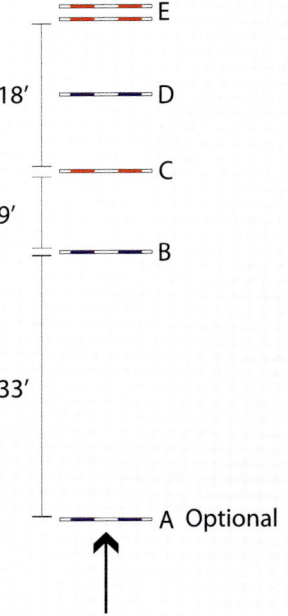

THE EXERCISES

83 /

When you're ready for the back rail of the oxer (Jump E), make sure it is in a breakaway cup. I always try to do this for safety.

Once Jump E is in, raise the jumps until they are an appropriate challenge for your horse. Personally, I max this exercise out at a 1.20-meter vertical and a 1.30-meter oxer with a 1.0-meter spread for the oxer.

As you are working through the exercise, make sure you have a good focus on straightness, as this is key. If you are struggling at all with straightness, don't be afraid to use straightening poles, either placed on the ground or propped up on the jump. And if you are struggling with finding the correct distance to the first ground pole, go ahead and add in Ground Pole A 33 feet away. While this may sound like it's making the exercise harder, it actually makes things easier. The 33-foot distance is enough room so if you struggle over the first pole, you have enough room to circle away from the line and try again. ◆

EXERCISE EXPERT

Coursework and Traditional Gymnastic

Melissa Hunsberger

of Melissa Hunsberger Equestrian in Boyce, Virginia

This exercise is a nice combination of traditional gymnastic work and more complex coursework. The difficulty can also be easily adjusted for horses and riders of all levels.

/ MATERIALS NEEDED

- 1 ground pole
- 10 jump poles
- 9 sets of standards

/ SETUP

- This exercise is best set on the centerline of your jumping area.

- The bending lines can be adjusted slightly to fit your space, but in general, your turns should not be too severe.

▽ **About the expert:**

A Level III ICP Certified Instructor, Melissa Hunsberger is based in Area II. She prides herself on education, with fun and safety being paramount. Melissa has many students in the area at all levels and instructed the Loudoun Hunt Pony Club for many years. She herself has competed through the CCI5* level with two horses she brought along from the beginning. ◆

/ WHY

One of the main reasons why I love this grid is because it is so adjustable, and it suits a lot of different types of horses and riders. For the lower-level pairs, it is a straightforward grid that perfectly introduces bending lines. For the more experienced pairs, it is a good way to combine traditional gridwork with some more complex coursework. Regardless of your level, there are infinite variations you can do to make it as complex or as simple as you want to suit your needs.

I think that any grid is great for allowing the rider to hone in on her position and focus on her horse's straightness. This particular grid has enough to do that forces the rider to keep looking ahead and, more importantly, *planning* ahead. Regardless of your level, the challenge of this exercise does not come from the height of the fences, but rather from the variations you can create as you work through it.

Due to the number of fences involved, it is best to do this grid when you have a friend on the ground to help. I learned the base of this grid from Phyllis Dawson when I worked at her Windchase Farm. While there, we would all take turns setting rails for other riders, and the same is true today. There's nothing better than a little free advice from the ground, especially when you're working on straightness, as it's often easier for the ground person to catch it when you're starting to drift than it is for you.

Finally, don't be afraid to adjust the distances based on what your horse needs. The distances described here are meant to be a trot-in grid, although it is fine to trot or canter in when you

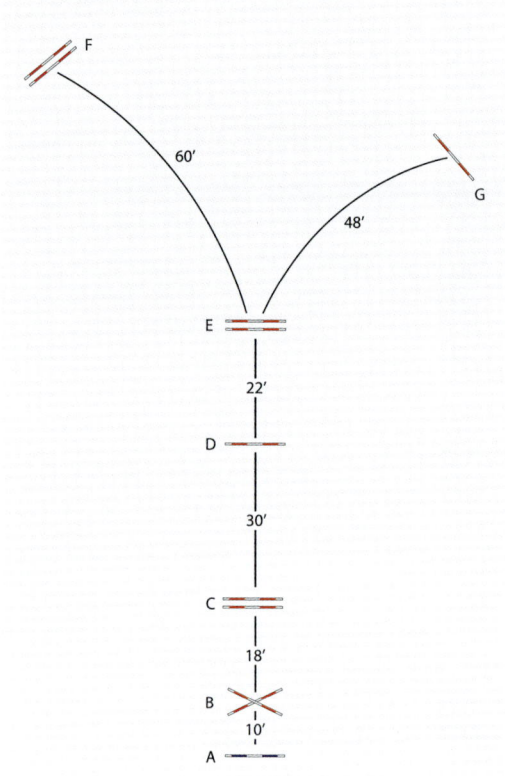

have just poles on the ground. I especially like to adjust the distances for the greener horses to give them confidence. And for the more experienced horses, you can adjust the distances to teach them better technique.

/ HOW

Before you start jumping, you should accomplish a few things on the flat that will set you up for success later. First, make sure that your horse is able to shorten and lengthen his stride within any gait. Of course, the degree of difference between the collection and lengthening will depend on the level of your horse. But the main thing is for your horse to understand that when you half-halt, he needs to come back; and when you put your leg on, he needs to go forward.

Additionally, throw in a little lateral work, whether it be simple leg-yields or more complex shoulder-ins, renvers, and half-passes. Regardless, the idea is to make sure your horse is actively listening to your aids so that you have the tools to hold him straight.

From here, start the exercise in one of three ways, depending on the level of your horse. I'll start with green horses and work up.

Put all the poles on the ground and have them walk, then trot, then canter through these a few times. Make sure you approach the rails from both the left and right side and try to approach the exercise from either side of the arena. This gives the horses a lot to look at, and since you're presenting the exercise to them from every direction while the poles are still on the ground, it makes your life easier later on, because they are less likely to be surprised.

Once your horse is quietly and confidently cantering through the poles, set up Jump B with the remaining poles on the ground. Then trot through the grid backward—that is from Jump E to A—a time or two so that the horse is comfortable with the "tunnel effect." Some horses can get a little claustrophobic or distracted in tight spaces, so this is the perfect time to expose them to this situation in a relaxed, schooling environment.

From here, turn back around so that you are approaching Jump B first again, with the poles in place at Jumps C, D, and E. And continue with building the grid. Before you put in Jump C, make sure that your horse is good and confident. If this means you have to trot and canter over just the cross-rail a dozen times before setting up the next fence, that's fine!

You can now start adding in Jumps D and E, jump by jump until the entire grid is built. I think that building the exercise up one jump at a time stops horses from having green moments. But if at any point your horse starts to have trouble, don't be afraid to take a step back until his confidence is back, then move on again.

For the most experienced horses, you can start with the whole grid set to a low height right away. Typically more experienced horses don't need you to build the exercise up bit by bit. Instead, by leaving the jumps quite low, you are simply warming up their jump muscles through what is nothing more than a cavalletti footwork exercise before getting to the real challenge of the exercise.

THE EXERCISES

Regardless of your horse's experience level, always continue on in a straight line after Jump E, and between Jumps F and G. Depending on your horse, you have two choices for what to do after Jump E: For more forward horses, utilize a halt transition on a straight line. Ideally you would halt before going between Jumps F and G, but if you don't, no big deal, just try again! For lazier type horses, land and make them go *forward* after Jump E, especially if they've gotten backed off through the grid. Then just rinse and repeat until your horse is keeping his rhythm through the entire exercise.

Once you have worked through the initial grid, it's time to move on to the fun stuff—the bending lines! Depending on the size of your arena, you can set the single fences at the distances outlined here, or you can move them in or out a stride.

When working Jumps F and G in, practice riding them in either a straight line or a bow. This gives you room to play with your striding.

For greener horses, make sure that they are jumping from the middle of Jump E to the middle of Jump F or Jump G. It's too easy for horses to have a runout if you let them drift away from the center of any jump.

The more experienced horses can play with making a straight line from the grid to the single fences. You will need to make sure that the tools are in place to make a pretty strong corridor between the leg and the hand to help with the straight line.

If your horse is easily navigating the lines to Jumps F and G, add in another element by circling back to the opposite single fence. For example, take your horse through the line, turn left to Jump F, and then roll back to the right to Jump G. The most experienced horses will then continue back through the grid from Jump E to Ground Pole A.

As with any grid, your job as the rider is to stay in the center of the horse. Grids are wonderful because they allow you to really fine-tune your position. And this grid is particularly good because it challenges you to keep your position through a small coursework exercise.

For this, keep the fences at or below your competition level. There's a lot to do, and you don't want to unnecessarily stress your horse. For less experienced horses, leave the single fences well below their competition level so that they aren't surprised. As you work through the exercise, keep your particular horse in mind and adjust accordingly. If he has a green moment, take a step back and reestablish his confidence before moving on. And as I mentioned earlier, having a knowledgeable set of eyes on the ground is very helpful; I always recommend having a groundperson when jumping. ◆

EXERCISE

Cavalletti and Coursework

EXPERT

Justine Jarvis

of Highgarden Farm in Frederick, Maryland

This is a great exercise to help prepare any rider for the show ring. It can be a very mental challenge for riders, and successfully navigating this exercise often gives just the right confidence boost before showing.

/ MATERIALS NEEDED

- 2 flower boxes, coops, or roll-tops

/ SETUP

- Try to set this up along the short side of your arena.

- Leave enough room between the obstacles and the rail that you can come off the rail in a rollback turn toward the jump. Keep in mind that the closer you stay to the rail, the harder your turn will be.

▽ **About the expert:**

A lifelong horsewoman, Justine has been competing up and down the East Coast for over 30 years, including trips to Devon, Capital Challenge, Harrisburg, and Washington International Horse Show. With experience in the hunters, jumpers, and equitation rings, Justine's program is well-rounded with students of all ages and levels. While based in Maryland, her team travels extensively and her students have picked up top finishes to earn them trips to Gittings Finals, MHSA Thoroughbred Invitational, Hunter Prix Finals, Devon, and Washington International Horse Show. ◆

www.highgardenfarm.com

- You can use most any filler for this exercise, whether it's flower boxes or coops or rolltops. The key is to *not* use standards.

/ WHY

This is one of my favorite exercises to help prep riders for the show ring. Two single obstacles without standards—whether it be 18-inch flower boxes or 3-foot roll-tops—on the short side of the arena is harder than anything most riders will see in competition. So if you're able to tackle this bounce with success and confidence, you know that you're capable of anything. I also like this exercise because it's not very difficult for the horse, meaning that you can practice it quite a bit without worrying about undue stress on your horse's legs. This is more of a mental challenge for riders than anything else. It's absolutely perfect for riders who tend to get a little anxious and need to feel like they've accomplished something.

While this exercise helps teach riders how to ride through a corner and keep their horse straight between their aids, more than anything else it teaches riders to "nerve up" and just do it. And while most riders strive for perfection, I encourage my students to allow themselves to make a mistake—as long as they learn from it on the other side of the mistake.

While it's nice to have an instructor on the ground, I want my riders to be able to think for themselves and self-critique their own riding. So if you're working on your own, give yourself a moment after each time through the bounce to ask yourself: What went well? What could have been better? And how could you make it better?

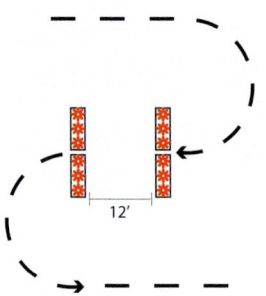

/ HOW

Before you even head to your first jump, make sure your horse is listening and turning well. Maybe include some smaller circles and figure eights in your warm-up. And remember to keep your expectations in line with your horse's abilities. My expectations of a green four-year-old are quite different than those of a seasoned campaigner.

If you've never done a bounce, you wouldn't want to start with this exercise. Instead, introduce your horse to bounces in a more traditional format with ground poles and standards, and gradually build it up. Make sure your horse knows what a bounce is before you present him with this "weird" bounce.

Once you are warmed up, start making your plan for your bounces. Remember that successful jumping rounds come from riding straight to your jumps out of good turns at a good pace. Sounds simple, right? But sometimes the simplest things can be the hardest.

When you've warmed up and have your plan, simply go directly to your bounces off a wide turn, and then off a short turn. With only two small jumps, there aren't a lot of steps.

You can play with the distance between the jumps depending on your horse. When you need help slowing your horse down, shorten the distance and teach him the rhythm of the exercise before widening the distance again.

If your horse is ducking to the inside as you come through the turn, it's likely you're using too much inside rein and not enough inside leg. If your horse is running to the outside, it's likely you're tipping in and not using your outside aids effectively. As I said already, it's okay to make mistakes, as long as you work to understand why they happened and fix them.

When you want to make this exercise harder, simply make the jumps bigger or narrower. I typically start with obstacles that are 8 feet wide, but you can challenge yourself by using more narrow jumps.

Give yourself a pat on the back when you've completed this successfully. If you can turn across the ring and ride into this exercise, you'll find anything at a horse show easy! ◆

EXPERT EXERCISE

Traditional Gymnastic

Stephanie Jenkins

of SRB Equestrian in Waterford, Virginia

▽ **About the expert:**

Based in Waterford, Virginia, Canadian Stephanie Jenkins (née Rhodes-Bosch) rose to fame with a team silver medal at the 2010 World Equestrian Games. With long-time partner Port Authority, Stephanie has earned multiple top Advanced finishes across the country at top venues such as The Fork CIC4*, Jersey Fresh CCI4*, Fair Hill CCI4*, and Kentucky CCI5*. Stephanie pulls from her extensive experiences to give each of her students and training horses a customized, positive learning experience. ◆

These are great exercises for horses and riders coming back to jumping after a little time off. The combination of ground poles and related distances gives both horse and rider something to think about without being too taxing.

/ MATERIALS NEEDED

- 5 ground poles
- 6 jump poles
- 6 sets of standards

/ SETUP

- The distances in this exercise can be adjusted to fit into your arena.

- It is recommended to have extra ground poles on hand in case you need to add one here or there.

GRID PRO QUO / *Margaret Rizzo McKelvy* /

- After setting up the exercise, put the jump poles to the side and leave only the ground poles in place.

/ WHY

This is one of my favorite exercises for horses just coming back into work after some time off, whether they were getting some scheduled vacation or unscheduled rehabilitation. With plenty of poles on the ground, Exercise 1 is a good exercise to remind horses of where to put their bodies. The rails aren't there to try to trip them up in an effort to sharpen them but instead to spell things out a bit and give them confidence. If your horse starts to rush a little, or lands in a heap, the ground poles help him (and you!) regain his center of balance. Consequently, if the rider gets off balance, the ground poles will make the horse's job twice as hard, as he is now having to not only keep his center of balance, but also adjust for his off-centered rider. So it's a great exercise of control for the rider.

Exercise 2 tests the skills you learned in the first exercise. Essentially, it's a challenge to see if you can keep the canter manufactured in Exercise 1 on your own. I tend to put five strides between the ground pole and the oxer because I find that it is just the right amount of space. Any more and you're lending yourself to getting flat, and any less poses no challenge. Putting these two exercises together will really encourage your horse to jump up and around the fences, which is just what you want when coming back into work.

/ HOW

Start Exercise 1 with all of the rails (Ground Poles A) on the ground. Let the horse—especially the young horse—walk through the ground poles, then trot through them.

PRO TIPS

- Overall, these jumps don't need to be big at all to make your point. In fact, if you have a horse that tends to rush, I would rather teach him to wait over smaller fences, than just raise the jumps in an effort to hold him off the fences. I suggest installing a verbal "Whoa" button before jumping anything. This may sound simple and silly to some, but it has come in handy many times in my competitive career.

  What I do is pick up my canter around the arena doing canter-walk and walk-canter transitions. Before doing any downward transition, I say "Whoa." Eventually your horse should put the verbal "Whoa" command together with slowing down a gear. When you're jumping, it is most helpful to use the "Whoa" command after your horse has taken off and is starting to put the landing gear down. Then he knows to land and go slowly, as opposed to landing and rushing.

THE EXERCISES

Ideally, you'll be walking and trotting through the rails on a soft, if not long, rein. The idea is to let the horse figure out his footwork on his own.

Once you've done this a few times, pick a soft connection at the canter. You don't want your horse to flounder around on a long rein, but you also don't want to be micromanaging. You can work on the rail, or on a circle, until you have the connection you want, then casually canter through the ground poles a few times.

Be sure to change direction each time you come through, and if your horse finishes on the incorrect lead, don't worry, just fix it through a simple or flying change, ideally before reaching the end of the arena.

Once you've warmed up sufficiently over the ground poles, put in Jump B first, as there are enough rails on either side to help you maintain your rhythm before and after the fence. You want to keep the same rhythm, and once you've accomplished this, add in Jump C, then Jump D, and finally Ground Pole E. If your rhythm gets quicker or slower at any point, just make your correction and try again.

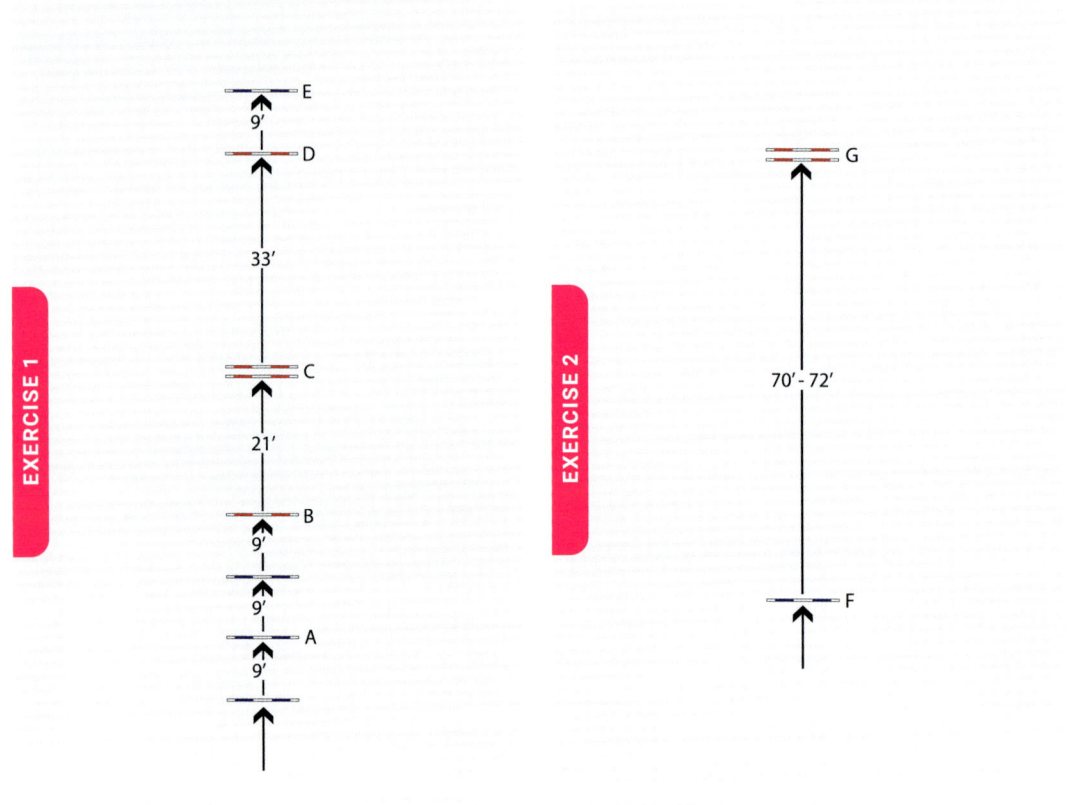

GRID PRO QUO / *Margaret Rizzo McKelvy* /

Once you're able to maintain your metronome rhythm not only through the grid, but also in your approach and departure, you're ready to move on to Exercise 2.

This is one of those exercises that is only as complicated as you make it. Simply put, you have Ground Pole F five strides before an oxer (Jump G). Your job as the rider is to be calm and patient, allowing your horse to find the rhythm and striding to the oxer.

Depending on your horse's fitness, it is often helpful to gradually raise Jump G until it is at your maximum comfort level. Being patient to a big oxer can be quite challenging for some riders, so use this as a time to school the challenge so that when you're faced with a big square oxer off a long approach in competition, you know exactly what to do! ◆

EXPERT EXERCISE

Cavalletti

Allison Kavey

of Rivendell Dressage in Millbrook, New York

▽ **About the expert:**

Allison Kavey is a CDI Grand Prix dressage rider who enjoys bringing horses up the levels. She works with dressage riders, eventers, and hunter/jumper riders with the shared goal of improving rider-horse communication through improved technique. She is a "process addict" who reminds herself and her riders the goal of good riding is better riding, and better riding comes from a commitment to the practice of dressage. Her clients range from adult amateurs to international riders, and she enjoys working with anyone who wishes to improve. ◆

This exercise looks like a lot on paper, but when you break it down into pieces, it is quite appropriate for horses and riders of all levels. You can practice it throughout the year to tune up your horse's footwork without overjumping him.

/ MATERIALS NEEDED

- 12 wooden ground poles and 12 blocks

OR

- 12 cavalletti

/ SETUP

- This can be set up in most arenas or flat fields, but try to center it in your area, with the 66-foot distance being from the center of the respective ground poles or cavalletti.

GRID PRO QUO / *Margaret Rizzo McKelvy* /

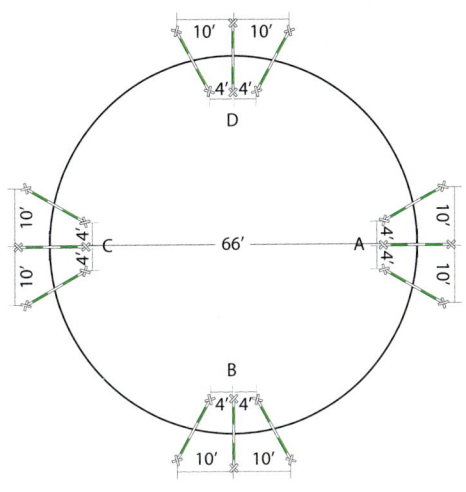

between both legs, as the rider needs to really pay attention to placing the horse to the appropriate step length along each rail.

I like to integrate transitions into the exercise as well, perhaps trotting clockwise through the poles at 3:00 (A) and 6:00 (B), then picking up a canter immediately following the final pole at 6:00 (B) and cantering the poles at 9:00 (C) and 12:00 (D). There is no need to make your cavalletti any higher than 6 inches as the exercise is challenging enough for most horses and riders without adding height.

This is also a great exercise to do on your own as it can be ridden at all three gaits and with plenty of variations without any need to get off and reset.

/ HOW

While this exercise can be done with as few as six poles or cavalletti, it's more fun when you have all twelve. And if you are using rails with blocks, alternate which side you raise up. For example, in Cavalletti Group A, the first and last rails would have the left side in a block, and the middle pole would have the right side in a block. And then you would alternate sides like this around your entire circle.

You should start this exercise at the lowest height or on the ground. The inside of the circle is spaced for a collected walk, the middle is set for a collected or working trot—your choice based on your level—and the far outside is set for a collected canter.

You can start in a variety of ways, depending on your horse, but it's always safe to start at the

- When setting your cavalletti groups, be sure to measure your distances both on the inside and outside to make sure everything is symmetrical.

- You can use either traditional cavalletti, or wooden rails with blocks to raise the height a bit.

/ WHY

One of the great things about this exercise is that it encourages consistency in rhythm and step, while allowing the rider and horse to work on improving their lift and push without overworking the horse's body. This series of cavalletti also requires excellent control of the horse walk then progress to the trot and canter. Here are a few variations (note that some of these have you traveling on the circle, while some have you pick up cavalletti groups on a straight line):

1. *Travel on the rail and pick off Cavalletti Group A and C located on the sides of your work area.*

2. *Make a 20-meter circle at either end of the arena, and only go through the Cavalletti Group B or D.*

3. *Make a serpentine in which you ride the half-circle of cavalletti (for example track right through Cavalletti Groups D, A, and B) and then change direction (after Cavalletti Group B) to leave the exercise.*

4. *Change directions within the circle, working on your change of bend and moving the horse from leg to leg in the process—this is great for testing your accuracy.*

5. *And, of course, go through all the sets of cavalletti on a single circle.*

As you work through the exercise you want to concentrate on being very consistent throughout. Start by picking a clear line and rhythm that you determine prior to getting to your first cavalletti, with the goal of maintaining it throughout. Then look at your own position. You should be equally as consistent and grounded in your lower legs. Be careful not to lean forward or lose your balance as your navigate the poles. Even with the poles at the lowest height possible, this exercise is a great position workout!

Also think about making sure that your horse is genuinely balanced between your legs and you are not using your reins to steer. You want to create and maintain a soft connection from your horse's hind end through the bridle, rather than allowing your horse to lean on you in any way.

Lastly, this exercise can be used to improve your horse's gaits throughout the circle. There should be no change in your horse's rhythm or balance as he goes through the exercise. He should move as well between the cavalletti groups as through them. ◆

EXERCISE EXPERT

Cavalletti

Ingrid Klimke

of Ingrid Klimke Stables in Münster, Germany

This is one of those easy-to-set-up exercises that you can utilize throughout the week without worrying about overtaxing your horse's legs. There are infinite ways to make these three cavalletti as difficult or as easy as you need them to be.

/ MATERIALS NEEDED

- 3 to 4 cavalletti

/ SETUP

- These can be set up anywhere in your arena provided they are on a straight line.

- If you do not have cavalletti, you can use jumps set to a low height.

▽ **About the expert:**

Ingrid Klimke is an international trainer of dressage, show jumping, and event horses, and currently competes for Germany as an event rider. She has appeared at four Olympics, from 2000 to 2012. With her horse Abraxxas, she won two gold medals in team eventing at the 2008 and 2012 Olympics. She placed seventh at the 2002 Dressage World Cup Final with the horse Nector van het Carelshof. In addition to a prolific competitive career, Ingrid has published several books, including *Training Horses the Ingrid Klimke Way* and *Cavalletti for Dressage and Jumping*. ◆

www.ingrid-klimke.de

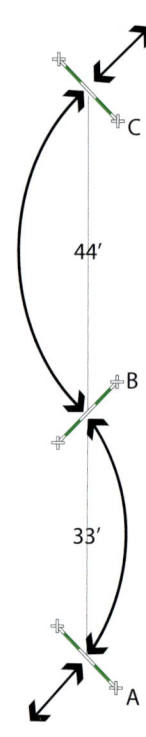

/ WHY

There is more than one way to improve your jumping, and they don't all involve actual jumps. I like to use cavalletti extensively in my training program and this "snake line" is something you will often find in my arena.

With only three to four cavalletti needed, this is something that is easy to set up, and since it doesn't take up a lot of room, you can just leave it up and still have plenty of room to work around it (although, I tend to integrate cavalletti into my everyday work).

/ HOW

As you begin this exercise, remember that the distances between the two sets of cavalletti are different. To warm up, you should just ride one arc of the serpentine line and canter over two cavalletti (for example, Cavalletti A to B, or vice versa) then change direction and ride the other arc over two cavalletti (Cavalletti B to C, or vice versa). When you're able to do both separately and smoothly, put all three cavalletti together.

You should have three canter strides between Cavalletti A and B, and four strides between Cavalletti B and C. It is important to count your strides and repeat the exercise until you are getting the proper number of strides between each cavalletti.

It is also important to change your canter lead over each cavalletti. To do so, you will have to change the bend to the new direction over the cavalletti so your horse lands on the correct lead.

GRID PRO QUO / Margaret Rizzo McKelvy /

If you want to challenge yourself, ride a straight line over the three cavalletti, which requires you to angle the approach to the first and last cavalletti. This changes your striding to two canter strides between Cavalletti A and B, and three strides between Cavalletti B and C.

When you are looking for an even bigger challenge and have a big enough arena, add a fourth cavalletti set 52 feet from your third cavalletti, which is ridden in five strides when riding the arc, or four strides when riding the straight line.

As you work through this exercise be sure to count out loud, which will help you get a feel for the rhythm and distances. Don't forget to give your horse a lot of breaks as this is a physically demanding exercise. ◆

EXPERT EXERCISE

Cavalletti and Coursework

Anne Kursinski

of Market Street in Frenchtown, New Jersey

About the expert:

Anne Kursinski is a five-time Olympian, two-time Olympic silver medalist, author, clinician, and international competitor. Her passion for the show ring and sport is strong. Along with competing and winning, she has been involved in the development and promotion of the sport. Through her Market Street facility in Frenchtown, New Jersey, Anne uses her great talents as a trainer and clinician to help riders achieve their goals. Her book *Anne Kursinski's Riding & Jumping Clinic* is a bestselling reference for those pursuing jumping disciplines. ◆

www.marketstreetinc.com

This exercise is perfect for riders who want to work on the rhythm and timing to their jumps. While this example utilizes one cavalletti in the center of the arena, you can adapt this to work over most any jump you have available to you.

/ MATERIALS NEEDED

- 1 cavalletti

OR

- 1 jump pole and 2 standards

/ SETUP

- While this example utilizes a single cavalletti in the center of your arena, you can get creative and utilize most any sort of jump for this exercise.

GRID PRO QUO / Margaret Rizzo McKelvy /

/ WHY

If you've ever come to one of my clinics, you've probably seen me work riders through this exercise. I like it for several reasons, including that a rider can set it up in her own arena and work on it outside of lessons. It also lets you work on your jumping without putting unneeded wear and tear on your horse's legs.

This exercise is all about the rhythm and timing to a jump. Counting out loud is also a mental exercise that many riders don't practice enough. And if you commit to practicing, you'll get it faster and it will only improve your riding. This exercise is like playing piano scales, but instead of scales, you're counting up to a jump.

The purpose of this exercise is to ride the rhythm and count your strides so that riding

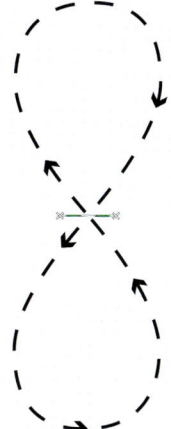

EXERCISE 1

EXERCISE 2

• PRO TIPS

One tip for successfully completing this exercise is to remember that it's better to start counting too early than too late. This way you aren't tempted to choke up on your horse to fit in your strides.

You will find as you practice this, your awareness of how far away you are from your obstacle will improve. As you work on your awareness, your ability to see your distance to a jump will improve. It's all about repetition and counting early.

THE EXERCISES

your jumps without disrupting your horse's rhythm becomes second nature. You don't want to adjust your horse's strides to fit your counting, which is why I always count up (one, two, three), as I believe that counting down (three, two, one) promotes backward riding.

/ HOW

Start by warming up at the walk and trot in a figure-eight pattern over your cavalletti or ground pole in the center of the arena as illustrated in Exercise 1. You will want to have a long approach, meaning that you need to angle your approach to the the obstacle slightly from left to right and then right to left.

When you pick up the canter, concentrate on feeling when your horse's feet hit the ground the last time before "takeoff" over your obstacle. At this moment, say, "One," out loud. This helps train your mind to count in time with your horse's footfalls.

As you approach your obstacle the next time, aim to start counting two strides before and say, "One, two," out loud before takeoff.

Continue to challenge yourself until you can successfully count up to your obstacle from eight strides away.

As you extend your counting from "one" all the way to "eight," remember it's okay to make a mistake. Simply just repeat your number until you can do it successfully. And don't forget to give your horse, and yourself, a few walk breaks, as this is a lot of cantering.

Remember your horse will find his own distance to a jump without a rider's help. So it's your job to simply ride the rhythm and allow him to do his job.

If you want to increase the challenge of this exercise, change your line so you are coming to your obstacle off short turns from the long side (think a rollback), as illustrated in Exercise 2. The key to this new pattern is to look at your jump early, and not start counting until you're looking at your obstacle. You'll quickly begin to recognize how many strides away from the jump you are, even if you're still in your turn. This means that you're more likely to follow your horse up to the obstacle, versus holding your horse back and choking them into a distance.

And as always, remember that if you make a mistake in your counting, simply try again. ◆

GRID PRO QUO / *Margaret Rizzo McKelvy* /

EXERCISE EXPERT

Traditional Gymnastic

Captain **John** *Ledingham*

of Maynooth, County Kildare, Ireland

This exercise works on developing better timing for both the horse and rider. The repetitive distances allow for riders to concentrate on their own position and horses to work on their own shape over the jumps.

/ MATERIALS NEEDED

- 5 ground poles
- 5 jump poles
- 4 planks
- 5 sets of standards
- 14 guide poles

/ SETUP

- This exercise requires a lot of materials and space to set up fully.

- If your arena cannot fit the entire exercise, you can simply use as many combinations as you can fit.

▽ **About the expert:**

Captain John Ledingham was a member of the Irish Army Equitation School until his retirement in 2002. He competed in the 1988 Seoul Olympics, three World Championships, three European Championships, and 63 Nations Cups for Ireland. He also was a three-time winner of the Hickstead Derby and the Hickstead Speed Derby, and four-time winner of the Royal Dublin Horse Show Puissance, setting a record of 7 feet 5 inches in 1987! Since his retirement, he has focused on coaching and travels the world teaching. ◆

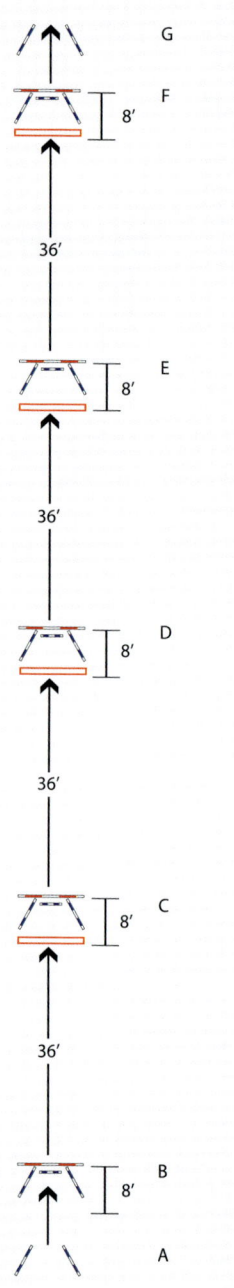

- The 4 planks will be used as ground poles. If you do not have planks available to you, use 2 ground poles put together to give yourself the width of a plank.

- After you place all your jumps, put all the poles to the side except for Jump B and your Guide Poles G.

/ WHY

I developed this canter grid to help improve a horse's timing in combinations. It is of utmost importance that a horse has the ability to shorten and lengthen his stride while not only staying straight, but also pushing off the ground.

Regardless of your discipline, this exercise also helps you as a rider work on your own timing. We all know that a proper canter means everything, and whether you're galloping down to a combination out on cross-country or coming into a triple combination in the jumper ring, this exercise helps you manufacture the right canter.

This exercise also helps the rider work on her own balance over a series of fences. This is so important because when you are in balance, it allows your horse to use his own body efficiently and effectively.

/ HOW

The first thing you will notice is that we're using planks as our placement poles. I like to place these 8 feet from the fence to make sure that the non-jumping stride is round and gets the horse to an effective takeoff place. The shape of the plank, combined with the distance, stops a horse from taking off too early if he finds the distances a challenge when the jumps get bigger.

To get started, set up your line of fences, but put all your planks and poles to the side, just leaving up your first jump and a chute of standards, along with the Guide Poles G at the very end after Jump F.

This entire exercise is quite long—144 feet in total—which makes it a great exercise to work on straightness. As you work your way through the exercise, make sure you go through the final guide poles every time.

You'll notice that Jump B *does not* have a placement plank but *does* have guide poles on the ground. You also have an entrance set of guide poles (Guide Poles A). The distance from Guide Poles A to Jump B can vary based on the dimensions of your arena, but the goal is to place them at a distance that encourages a straight approach to Jump B.

After you've warmed up over Jump B a few times, add in Jump C, complete with the plank placement.

Continue to build up the rest of the exercise until you have all five verticals (Jumps B, C, D, E, and F) in place.

As you work your way through the exercise, make good use of your guide poles. You can make them as narrow or wide as necessary. Just make sure they are effective for your particular horse. And if you have a horse that's a little claustrophobic at first, keep them wide, and then narrow them if needed. One of the keys to this exercise is to always monitor your horse's reaction to the questions you're asking him.

And for yourself, pay particular attention to your leg position and your ability to recover quickly on landing. Position is everything! ◆

EXPERT EXERCISE

Turning

Mary Lisa Leffler

of Rolling Acres Show Stables in Brookeville, Maryland

About the expert:

Mary Lisa Leffler has been a professional rider since 1994. Prior to her professional career, she was an accomplished junior and amateur rider. A few of her Adult Amateur highlights include retiring the Amateur-Owner hunter championship trophy at Devon and Harrisburg. As a professional rider, Mary has broken into the Grand Prix jumper ranks as well as maintaining her superior hunter rider status. She has won more than 25 Grand Prix events. As a trainer, Mary has students successfully competing in the children's and adult jumpers as well as the junior jumpers and hunters. ◆

www.rollingacresshowstables.com

This exercise combines the idea of being straight while jumping off a turn. Regardless of your discipline or level, this is a great way to work on those skills, which will only help you in the show ring.

/ MATERIALS NEEDED

- 3 jump poles
- 3 sets of standards

/ SETUP

- You can set this up most anywhere in your arena where you have room, but it is best set up in a corner if you have the space.

- Don't overcomplicate this exercise with a lot of jump filler, instead just use plain jump poles and standards.

/ WHY

I like to use this exercise both for my more inexperienced

GRID PRO QUO / Margaret Rizzo McKelvy /

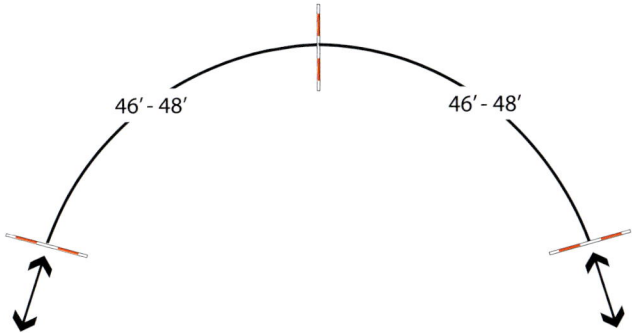

students as well as my seasoned competitors. For the less seasoned horse and rider pair, this teaches them their leads and makes turning easier. When they can successfully navigate this exercise, they will feel more confident jumping off turns in the competition arena.

For my more experienced jumper students, I've found that they've often become so used to jumping off turns, they've forgotten how to keep their horse straight. And regardless of whether your jump is off a turn or has a long, straight approach, your horse needs to be straight between your aids. When your horse is crooked, you will likely start dropping rails. This exercise combines the idea of being straight, while also being on a turn.

/ HOW

If you're a less experienced rider jumping under 2-foot-6-inch fences, start by letting your horse walk, trot, and canter through the exercise with the poles on the ground. Focus on staying in the middle of all the jumps as you go through. If you're struggling with your accuracy, you can use striped poles, or simply put a piece of duct tape around the middle of the jump pole so you can clearly see the target.

After you've warmed up over the ground poles, build up your exercise one jump at a time, starting with heights below your competition level.

If you're a more experienced rider who regularly jumps over 2 feet 6 inches, you can go ahead and start with all the jumps in place at a low height. Think of the jumps as small cavalletti that you're using to warm up your and your horse's jump muscles.

Regardless of how you start this exercise, as you work your way through it, think about controlling your own body and about how your horse feels as he works his way through the jumps. While the rules stay the same as your jumps start being built up, in that your horse needs to remain between your aids and jumping through the center of each jump, you should be thinking about how your horse is using his body over and between each jump. Really take the time to think about the nuances of your particular horse. Does he like to drift to the left? And if so, does he drift through his shoulders or through his haunches? Or does he like to lower, or raise his head the last step before a jump?

All these things tell you something about your horse, and the more you know about him, the more you can help him be successful. This requires a lot of self-reflection, but it will pay off in the end! ◆

EXERCISE EXPERT

Cavalletti and Traditional Gymnastic

Boyd Martin

of Windurra in Cochranville, Pennsylvania

These exercises work on the rider's ability to adjust her horse through a variety of distances and help make sure she has all the tools she needs when competing.

▽ **About the expert:**

/ MATERIALS NEEDED

- 12 ground poles (optional)
- 2 cavalletti
- 10 jump poles
- 10 sets of standards

One of the leading event riders of today, Boyd Martin has competed at three Olympic Games, three World Equestrian Games, and two Pan American Games where he's won two team gold medals and one individual gold medal. He has competed at all the world's top events, and recently won the inaugural Maryland CCI5*. Boyd and his wife Silva, a German-born Grand Prix dressage rider, own and operate their farm Windurra USA in Cochranville, Pennsylvania. ◆

/ SETUP

- These three exercises can be set up anywhere in your jumping arena.

- If you're tight on space, you can set the lines up on the diagonals to give yourself more room.

www.boydandsilvamartin.com

THE EXERCISES

- If your horse is on the greener side, consider using ground poles on either side of all the jumps to make clear ground lines.

/ WHY

In the sport of modern eventing, show jumping course designers are getting craftier with the design of their courses. With this in mind, these particular exercises work for anyone looking to improve the show jumping phase. Regardless of your discipline, course designers will sometimes set "traps" that lure riders into letting their horses get strung out, which often results in horses pulling rails. The really crafty designers often have combinations set on open distances that encourage the horses to get strung out, then follow these open combinations with upright fences, such as a tall vertical or plank jump.

What this means is that to jump these fences, your horse must be physically adjustable and you as a rider need to be mentally adjustable. The three exercises outlined in these diagrams are all good exercises in adjustability. Riders of any level can use them, with just a few modifications. Likewise, they are appropriate for horses of any level, as long as you keep the height of the fences appropriate for their current education.

/ HOW

When warming up for this type of jump school, ride your horse in a light seat and really encourage him to have an open and forward canter. You can do this exercise in a big arena or jump field, but you can certainly still accomplish what you need in a smaller arena or indoor. Depending on your riding space and your horse, you may need to work a little harder to get an open canter.

Once you establish a nice, forward canter, bring your shoulders back a little, touch down in the saddle lightly, and ask your horse to rock back and shorten his stride. More experienced horses should demonstrate a pretty dramatic difference in their length of stride and should also be able to maintain the shortened canter for a period of time before you lighten your seat again and ask for the open canter.

Slightly less experienced horses probably won't show as big of a difference in their length

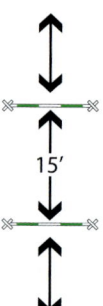

EXERCISE 1

15'

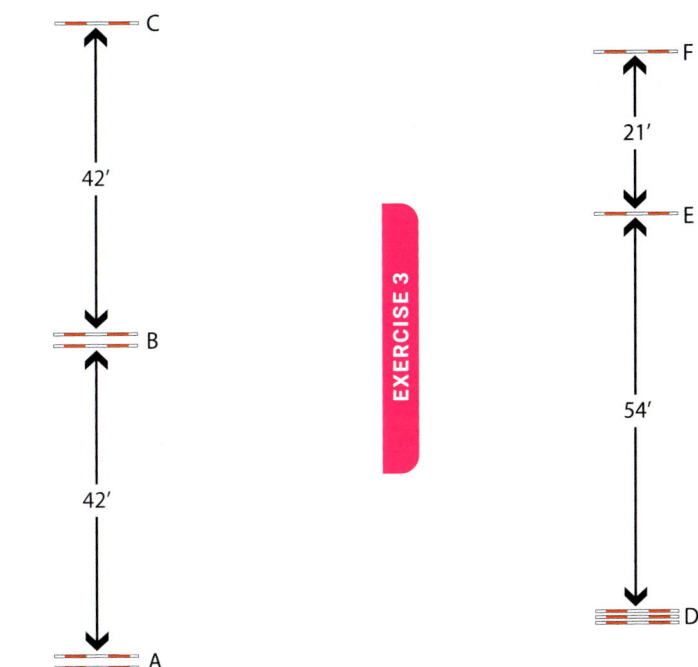

of stride, nor will they be able to maintain it for very long. But the most important thing for the younger horses is that they try to acknowledge that you are asking them for something different. This will be the key to laying the foundation for an adjustable horse later on.

Once you feel your horse is fairly adjustable at the canter, you can start with Exercise 1. The 15-foot distance is not quite a bounce, but also not quite a full stride, but with some adjustability it can act as either one. When you start this exercise, approach it in your open canter and treat it as a bounce. If your horse makes a bit of a mess of the exercise the first time through, don't worry! Just approach it again in the same canter until he is easily bouncing the exercise.

From there, make a circle and shorten your horse's stride. Now approach Exercise 1 again, looking for a deep, waiting distance, and fit a full stride between the cavalletti. Again, if you don't succeed the first time, don't worry! Just try again. This can be a hard concept for some horses—and riders—so if this is the first time you are trying an exercise like this, this warm-up exercise might end up being your entire jump school for the day, and that's okay. Simply come back to the exercise the next day and build from there.

THE EXERCISES

The eventual goal with this warm-up exercise is for your horse to gain the understanding that he needs to jump some fences forward and open, and some fences on a shortened stride and on his hind end. You will find that it is very easy to go from a shorter stride to a longer one, but much harder to go from longer to shorter. So you will probably have to work on this a bit harder. I have been very lucky to ride with some of the great jumper riders of our generation, and they all stress how your horse needs to be adjustable like an accordion.

Once you are satisfied with your warm-up over the cavalletti, move on to Exercise 2 with the three-stride line of oxers and vertical. To start off, set the fences slightly lower than your competition level. Approach the exercise so you are doing Jump C first and then the oxers (Jumps B and A). As I mentioned earlier, it is much easier to go from a shorter stride to a longer one, so in this case, you will do your "careful jump" first, then encourage your horse to get big and open over Jumps B and A. Then simply turn the exercise around and jump Jump A first to Jumps B and C. As expected, you want a big, scopey jump over the oxers, then steady your horse to the upright vertical.

Keep in mind when setting up that you need to design the fences in a way your horse will easily understand them. For the greener horses, give them really good ground lines, especially at the vertical. My goal is to inspire confidence, and making them too tricky does nothing to improve your horse's confidence. However, make sure that if your horse does decide to run through your hand at any point, he has a ground rail. The majority of horses want to be careful and do their job, so it is our job to properly educate them; often, especially when the horse is younger, having a rail teaches him to be careful without scaring or hurting him in any way.

If your horse is having trouble with the exercise and pulling a lot of rails, you can do two things. First, make the oxers (Jumps A and B) into ascending oxers, which makes them a little easier for the horse to read. If you are running into trouble at the vertical (Jump C), set two poles into a "V" on the vertical, which encourages him to slow down. It will probably also make him jump a bit bigger over the vertical, so be prepared for that.

Remember that the eventual goal for you as the rider is to do this exercise so that you are not using too much hand. Keep in mind your warm-up exercise where you have a light seat for your open canter, which is what you will want for your oxers. And then sit up tall for your shortened canter, which is what you need for your vertical. You can also train your horse to respond to a little bit of your voice aid by training him to go forward off a cluck, and slow down with a "whoa."

Depending on your horse's education level, you can either end your jump school here, or raise the fences to your competition height and try again. Remember to never be afraid to "quit while you're ahead," especially when this is the first time that you're attempting this type of adjustability exercise. It's better to end a little early than to run into trouble when your horse is tired.

Exercise 3 is one I don't introduce until my horses and students are competing at Training Level or above, which is 3 feet 3 inches. This exercise is similar to Exercise 2, but a bit harder with the longer distance between the triple bar (Jump D) and the first vertical (Jump E), and then the shorter distance to the final vertical (Jump F). The concept remains the same though, and you should start by approaching Jump F first, then opening the stride for the triple bar. When this goes well, flip the exercise around, which includes adjusting your triple bar for the new direction. Then canter down over your triple bar (Jump D) and steady for the in-and-out with the verticals.

As a rider, your biggest goal is to be able to adjust your horse without your hand. The more upright you make your position, the more your horse should rock back and steady himself. A good visual to keep in mind is that of a dressage rider doing a pirouette. And for the more forward, open distance, you should be in a light seat. All these changes should be very discreet so when you're at a show and your horse feels you move around, he knows what you are expecting him to do. ◆

EXPERT EXERCISE

Cavalletti

Caroline Martin

of Caroline Martin Eventing in Springtown, Pennsylvania

▽ **About the expert:**

Ever since Caroline Martin won individual gold at the North American Junior and Young Rider Championships in 2014 on Quantum Solace, she has not looked back. Her experience grew along with her determination to represent the United States internationally. Caroline has already represented her country on multiple Nation's Cup Teams and topped annual leaderboards countless times. ◆

www.caroline-martin-eventing.com

Regardless of whether you're in the middle of competition season or enjoying the off season, this cavalletti exercise will be useful. This exercise doesn't take up a lot of room, so it's a great one to have set up to utilize in multiple rides throughout the week.

/ MATERIALS NEEDED

- 5 cavalletti

/ SETUP

- Setting up cavalletti on a bending line can be a bit of a challenge, so take your time and utilize a measuring stick or tape.

- Once in place, be sure to double check the inside, middle, and outside distances until they are just right.

GRID PRO QUO / *Margaret Rizzo McKelvy* /

/ WHY

There are many reasons why I love using cavalletti throughout the year, but the main one is that they help you practice seeing your stride without taxing your horse's legs. Not everyone has the option of jumping several horses a week, so it can be hard to find that balance between being able to practice your jumping enough and not over-jumping your horse. I find that cavalletti work is the perfect answer to this!

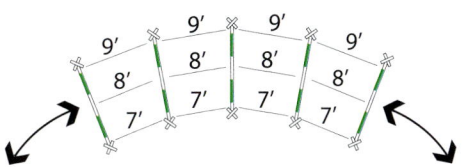

This particular setup is great for horses of every level and I use it often with every horse in my barn, from the green four-year-olds to the advanced campaigners. It not only helps improve their rideability, it also helps improve their cadence.

As mentioned, setting up cavalletti on a bending line can be a bit challenging, so don't be afraid to pull out your measuring tape, enlist the help of a friend, and really take your time. The distances slightly increase from the inside to the outside of the circle so you can utilize them at the trot and the canter, making this setup multi-purposeful for your flatwork ride.

/ HOW

Regardless of the age or level of your horse, always walk him through the inside track of the cavalletti a few times to get things started. As soon as your horse is calmly walking through cavalletti on a quiet connection, start trotting through center of them. And when you're ready to introduce the canter, stay to the outside, but gradually move him toward the inside to make him work a little harder.

For lower-level horses, the main goal is to try to get the horse to really work over his back and stretch into the cavalletti. You can leave the cavalletti on the ground, and just repeat the exercise until the horse is relaxed enough to really let go while working over the cavalletti.

For lower-level riders, you want to be able to start to feel the cadence in the trot. You can also learn how your body affects your horse by posting higher and lower and seeing how that changes your horse's way of going.

When it comes to cantering, you are simply looking for your horse to be able to cruise through the cavalletti while you are in a half-seat.

As a rider, practice getting deep to the base of the first cavalletti. This can sometimes make riders feel uncomfortable, but it's a good thing to

THE EXERCISES

practice. The key though is to not use your reins to try to find that deep distance; instead, sit squarely in the saddle, using your core to control your horse's length of stride and let your horse come up to you. Inevitably, when you do this, your horse will start to learn that a slightly longer distance isn't the way to go.

As you progress in experience, start to raise the cavalletti, and incorporate transitions to increase the difficulty of the exercise. The key to making the most of this simple exercise is to keep changing things up. Fit in as many transitions as are appropriate for your horse before and after the cavalletti. And be really strict with yourself about not only where your transitions will be, but where you're tracking across the cavalletti. If you want to do a transition every five strides, then do one every five strides—don't let your horse convince you that you can only do transitions every six, seven, or eight strides.

Try to set yourself up for success whenever possible. When it comes to these transitions there are two approaches to creating a successful circle of transitions. The first is to start with a *very* doable goal for the number of strides between transitions. With green horses or riders, start with 10 strides and go down from there. And again, keep your expectations realistic, so don't try to go from transitions every 10 strides to transitions every five strides in one training session. Work up to it!

The other approach to setting yourself up for success is to start with walk-halt transitions then increase the difficulty from there. So once you have the walk-halt transitions mastered, move on to walk-trot transitions, and so on, until you can do halt-walk-trot-canter-trot-walk-halt every four to five strides. Again, this doesn't have to happen in one training session, but instead can be a goal for yourself for a season.

Another rule to keep in mind is to not let your horse wobble between the rails. This means that if you're aiming for the inside line, don't let your horse drift out on the circle. This is where using striped cavalletti can come in handy because it helps give you a visual of where you want to be. They also help when doing this exercise with friends because you can tell others when they are drifting one way or the other, as it can sometimes be hard to recognize this when you're riding.

Being really strict with yourself on things like your transitions and line only help you when you start jumping. And again, the beauty of practicing this over cavalletti is that you're keeping your horse's mind busy, and challenging yourself as a rider, without taxing the horse's body too much. ◆

GRID PRO QUO / Margaret Rizzo McKelvy /

EXERCISE EXPERT

Traditional Gymnastic

Sinead Maynard

of Copperline Farm in Citra, Florida

These are great exercises for riders who want to focus on their own position. They also have an element of footwork that will help teach your horse a bit about his own responsibility over fences.

/ MATERIALS NEEDED

- 4 ground poles
- 5 square jump poles
- 5 sets of standards

/ SETUP

- None of these exercises take up a lot of room, so you can set them all up at once or you can have a ground person adjust things as you move through the exercise.

- While square jump poles are preferable, you can utilize your regular jump poles if that is all you have available.

▽ **About the expert:**

Sinead Maynard (née Halpin) is an international competitor and trainer and has been riding at the Advanced Level since 1999. In 2011, Sinead earned and maintained her spot on the world stage, proving to be a top competitor as well as a class ambassador of the sport by placing third in her first five-star at the Kentucky Three-Day Event. Based at Copperline Farm in Citra, Florida, which she owns with her husband, fellow eventer Tik Maynard, Sinead is an ICP Level II certified instructor and enjoys teaching students of all levels and ambitions. ◆

www.copperlineequestrian.com

/ WHY

There are many reasons why this is one of my go-to exercises for my jump schools. While it seems simple on paper, it's a great exercise for teaching rider responsibility while focusing on her position and also teaching horse responsibility with a focus on footwork.

From an instructor's point of view, I like teaching with this exercise because it's a good way for the rider to feel confident and learn that mistakes happen; they aren't always bad and the rider can handle it. The simplicity and repetitiveness of the exercise allows the rider to concentrate solely on her position and accuracy, without having to worry about an entire course of jumps.

From a trainer's point of view, I like riding over this exercise for many of the same reasons as I like teaching with it. It's a great way for horses to work on their footwork without making things too complicated. The key to correctly using a square rail is to never make the jump so high that if the horse makes a mistake it will be bad. The purpose of using a square rail is to make it so that when the horse gets to a jump a little wrong, he is encouraged to be clever in order to leave the rail up.

Regardless of whether you're aiming for your first local show or your first championships, this exercise will undoubtedly teach you something.

/ HOW

Once you are properly warmed up, start by letting your horse trot through Exercise 1 with all the rails on the ground. If you're riding a less experienced horse, let him trot through the rails a few times before making a small vertical.

Gradually raise the vertical as appropriate for your level. The focus should be on the rider's position and the horse's footwork, not the height of the jump.

After each time through the exercise, land and halt, then do a turn-on-the-forehand before heading back to the same vertical from the opposite direction.

On paper, trotting a small vertical should be easy. But anyone who regularly practices this will tell you that it's very easy to jump ahead or get left behind when trotting jumps.

EXERCISE 1

GRID PRO QUO / *Margaret Rizzo McKelvy* /

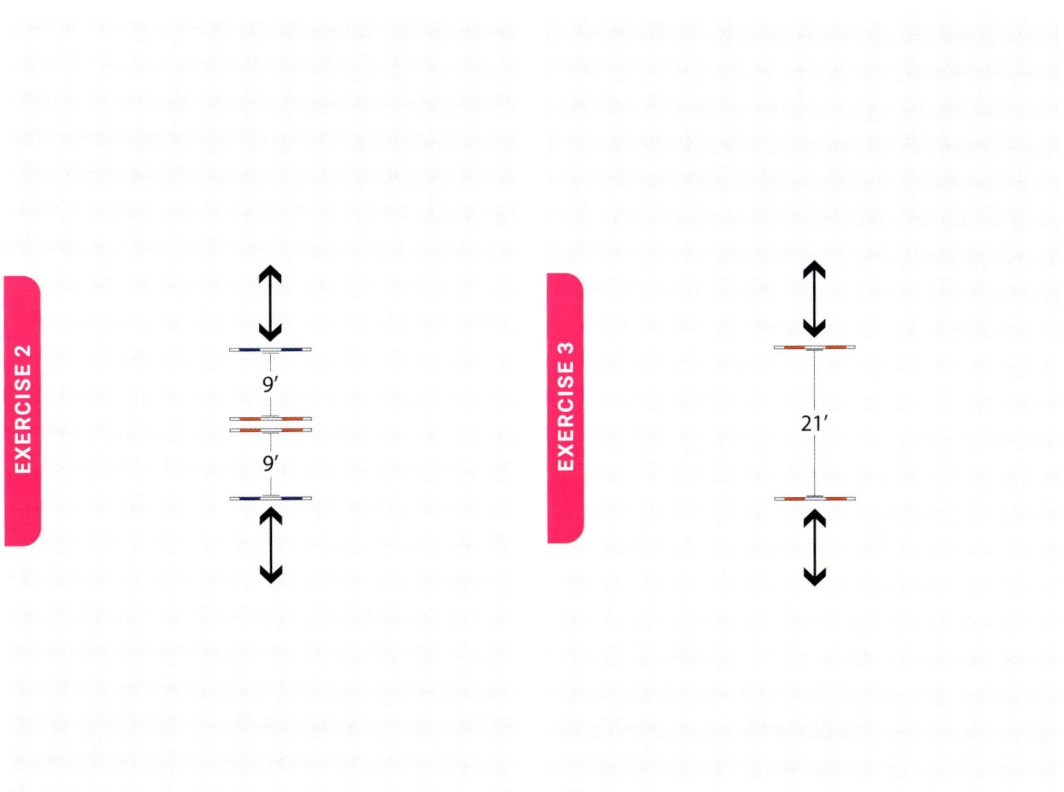

The best way to work out the kinks is to focus on creating a nice, rhythmic trot well before you turn to your jumps. And then simply focus on maintaining your perfect trot to the jump, rather than worrying about getting to the perfect distance.

If you're still having trouble staying with your horse through this trot fence exercise, there's one thing that tends to really help my students. Simply do not look at the jump! The more you stare at the jump, the more you anticipate the takeoff. You're not going to see your stride at a trot fence, so stop trying. The best thing to do is to look past the jump once you're on your line and just feel the jump come to you.

Before you move on to the next exercise, you want to be able to reliably land on either lead after your vertical. If you have a horse that tends to always land on one lead, do a figure eight over the vertical to encourage him to switch leads. If he is persistent in wanting to always land on one lead, first try to figure out why. Ask yourself, "Is my horse uncomfortable physically somewhere? Am I crooked in the saddle, causing my horse to compensate? Or, is it a training issue that needs to be corrected?"

THE EXERCISES

Regardless of the reason, don't expect to fix this—or any—issue in one training ride. As long as you're making progress in the right direction, you should be happy!

The next step is to take the vertical and make it into an oxer, as illustrated in Exercise 2, with a ground pole 9 feet in front of it, making it a cantering exercise.

Again Exercise 2 comes down to rider and horse responsibility. It's a common flaw for the rider to be overprotective and hold her horse off the pole, which causes you to end up riding a bit backward. All this means is that the rider has her priorities wrong, which isn't the end of the world, but this is a great exercise for showing you the importance of concentrating on finding a good rhythm and letting that carry you to your ground pole.

What you're looking to accomplish with your horse can dictate the type of oxer you set up. When your horse is on the greener side, keep it simple with an ascending oxer. When your horse is more experienced, you can make a small square oxer. Or, if your horse has a tight back, you can make a wider oxer, or even add a ground pole 9 feet on the landing side.

Straightness issues tend to pop up when you start cantering the oxer. While I will sometimes put V rails on the jump—always starting wide—riders should always remember that so much can be fixed with a good landing. So if you make it a priority to land in a straight line, it will carry over to your approach.

After you're comfortably and confidently doing these first two exercises you should have accomplished two things:

1. *From the trot exercise (Exercise 1), you're looking to become more in sync with your horse, and you want to have the horse-rider responsibilities worked out.*

2. *From the canter exercise (Exercise 2), you're looking for what shape you need from your horse, and gathering more information about your horse and how he jumps.*

Every horse is different, and some may need to spend more time doing the trot exercise while others may need to spend more time doing the canter exercise.

The next step is to take the oxer from Exercise 2 and turn it into a 21-foot one-stride, as illustrated by Exercise 3, with the second vertical quite a bit higher than the first one and with no ground line. Your second vertical should be a level higher than your competition level. This is a lot of footwork though, so make sure your horse can handle the height that you're competing at first before raising the jump.

This simple line using square rails tests the carefulness of your horse. And by taking the "base" away from the second vertical, the horse naturally wants to be more careful.

I tend to only jump through Exercise 3 twice before calling it a day. But if I'm looking to increase the challenge for my upper-level horses, I will simply play around with my approach, varying it from a short approach to a long one.

At the end of the day, the horse's responsibility is to jump well and the rider's responsibility is direction. Straightness and rhythm go hand in hand. You have to learn to trust the rhythm, trust your connection, and trust your responsibilities. And in this case, once you're two to three strides out, let the exercise do the work and have the confidence to stay in the middle of your horse and let him sort through the exercise. ◆

EXPERT EXERCISE

Groundwork and Traditional Gymnastic

Tik Maynard

of Copperline Farm in Citra, Florida

▽ **About the expert:**

A lifelong horseman, Tik Maynard is based in Citra, Florida, with his wife, fellow eventer Sinead Maynard, at their Copperline Farm. His business combines eventing and natural horsemanship, with students of every level and discipline. He recently published his first book, *In the Middle Are the Horsemen*. ◆

www.copperlineequestrian.com

This super exercise works on adjustability and rideability. The combination of groundwork and actual riding makes it a fun exercise for the off season, as well as something fun to do with your barnmates.

/ MATERIALS NEEDED

- 2 ground poles
- 2 cones

/ SETUP

- This exercise can be set up most anywhere, even outside in a nearby field.

- The 60-foot distance is a suggestion and can be adjusted to fit your space.

GRID PRO QUO / Margaret Rizzo McKelvy /

/ WHY

While on paper you may think that this exercise is overly simple, I find it is the perfect thing to work on during winter months to help prepare for the upcoming show season. I'm a big believer in training my horses—and students—in a systematic manner. This is a great exercise to set up on your own and practice in between lessons. Even better, get a group of friends together and make a game of it.

I developed this exercise to help teach my horses and students adjustability and rideability. As riders, we need to know what stride length our horse is on at any given time. This is important so when we're at a show we're able to adjust to any stride length the course designer is asking for. Being able to practice smoothly and quickly changing stride length throughout this exercise will help you at shows because your horse will be more adjustable and more rideable. And as a rider you will have the confidence to know that your horse is capable of any adjustability question you may face.

The great thing about this exercise is that you can set it up anywhere. If you're lucky to live where there's open space to ride, you can set it up in a field and use the terrain to add a little difficulty to the exercise. But I suggest starting out with setting this up in your arena. As you get comfortable with this exercise you can even set it up using a bank, cross-country jump, or a stadium fence as one of your poles. There are an infinite number of ways to make this exercise easier or harder.

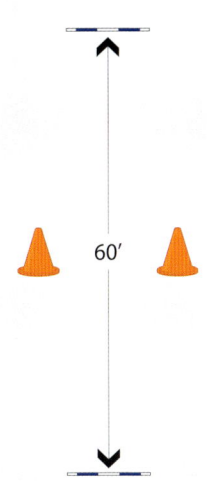

As you work through this exercise, I encourage you to challenge yourself, but never be afraid to back up a step if needed.

/ HOW

As you work through the exercise keep the following three priorities in mind:

1. *Is your horse safe at the end?*

2. *Are you safe at the end?*

3. *Is your horse more relaxed at the end than at the beginning? Your horse needs a certain level of relaxation in order to learn.*

This exercise can be built up in 15 progressive steps:

1. *Lead your horse in hand over the poles. You should be able to do this on a "loose rein," meaning he should calmly walk next to you back and forth over the ground poles a few times.*

2. *Walk over the poles mounted on a long rein. Again, your horse should be able to walk calmly over the poles. No stress. Even from the beginning, you want to make sure you're going over the center of each pole, which is why there are cones in the center to help test your straightness.*

3. *Walk 1, Trot 2: Regardless of the level of connection you have in the bridle—which should coincide with your level of training—you should simply pick up a quiet trot after walking over the first pole.*

4. *Trot 1, Walk 2: This is where some people can get caught up. Sixty feet is a long time to make a good downward transition, so don't rush it.*

5. *Trot both poles: Again, regardless of the level of connection you have in the bridle, just trot through the poles with your goal being to keep a quiet, consistent rhythm throughout.*

6. *Trot 1, Canter 2: This is a great way to practice your upward canter transitions by asking for the transition over the first pole. Or do the transition halfway between the two poles.*

7. *Canter 1, Trot 2: Just like your trot-to-walk transitions, remember you have plenty of time to make a transition.*

8. *Canter both poles: Whether you're in a half-seat or full-seat, your only goal here is to confidently canter over both poles. If you have trouble keeping your canter lead over both poles, try to think about going over the poles in an oval shape, rather than a square.*

9. *Canter both poles and count your strides. This is where it comes in handy to do this exercise with friends as you can help each other count strides.*

10. *Consistently get five strides: Challenge yourself to get five even, 10-foot strides between the two poles. The extra 10 feet is for takeoff and landing.*

11. *Alternate between five and six strides, four times in a row. The key to being able to alternate between two stride lengths is planning. You will quickly learn that you cannot solely rely on your reins to make these adjustments. Use your seat and leg to also help you adjust your stride, and think about changing the balance before you change the speed.*

12. *Get the following pattern: five, six, seven, six, five strides. The challenge here is to keep compressing your horse's stride, then immediately lengthen it back up.*

13. *Get the following pattern: four, five, six, seven, six, five, four strides. This is just a repeat of the previous exercise, but a slightly bigger challenge.*

14. *Get the following pattern: four, seven, four, seven. While the previous two were gradual transitions between stride length, this is more of a challenge to immediately change from four to seven strides.*

15. *Get creative! Set up the exercise in the center of your arena and try alternating directions each time with a flying change over the second pole. Make the exercise even harder by adding more strides or make them into jumps. Set this up outside and use terrain. Or try this using skinny rails.*

I like to use these steps as one gauge for when my horses and students are ready for a certain level. I tend to require my students to be able to get through Step 10 before competing at 2 feet 7 inches; Step 11 before competing at

PRO TIPS

- As mentioned earlier, I try to take a very systematic approach when teaching my students about eventing, and I believe that it starts on the ground. So before you even get your horse from the field, head out to your arena to set up your two ground poles. If you're inexperienced with setting fences, this is a great way to start.

  Measure out 60 feet with your tape measure then walk it out. It should be 20 of your 3-foot steps, and if it's not, simply keep practicing it until it walks easily for you. Nearly all stadium courses are based on a 12-foot stride. So this 60-foot exercise works out to four strides, with the extra 12 feet being for landing and takeoff.

  Remember, this particular exercise has 15 steps. As you work through the steps, if you run into a problem with any of these steps, back up a step. Don't simply keep trying at the current step. It's much more productive to take a step back, re-master that and then proceed forward again.

2 feet 11 inches; Step 12 before competing at 3 feet 3 inches; Step 13 before competing at 3 feet 7 inches; and Step 14 before competing at 3 feet 9 inches.

I cannot stress enough that if your horse is having any trouble, take a step back until he can do the previous step in a relaxed manner. I'm looking for the horse's mouth to be closed, his tail to be quiet, and for him to be able to keep a rhythm.

If your horse is having trouble relaxing with you on his back, work him in hand over the poles until he is ready to try again with you mounted. If your horse is getting anxious when you try to get him on the bit, go back to riding on a relaxed rein. I don't even begin to ask a horse to jump until he can walk, trot, and canter around—both in an arena and outside—on a relaxed rein.

Finally, spend some time watching your horse's ears while you're riding. They should be fairly relaxed and even flopping while you're hacking and flatting. And when you start jumping, his eyes and ears should look to the jump. Your horse should briefly check in with his rider in the turn before the jump, then think ahead to the jump in front of him. Your challenge as a rider is to see if you can communicate with your horse without interfering with his job. And the best way to do this is practice, practice, practice over these ground poles. ◆

EXERCISE EXPERT

Cavalletti and Traditional Gymnastic

Jenni McAllister

of Team McAllister in Dunnellon, Florida

This versatile exercise helps teach the rider the balance needed between the leg and rein aids. Quality transitions are the key to this exercise.

▽ About the expert:

/ MATERIALS NEEDED

- 4 ground poles
- 2 cavalletti

/ SETUP

- The distances between the ground poles and cavalletti are only suggestions and can be adjusted to fit your space.

- If you do not have cavalletti, you can use jumps set at a low height.

/ WHY

I first learned this exercise over 20 years ago, and I have kept it in my program for a good

Jenni Martin McAllister is an accomplished Grand-Prix-level professional show jumper. She has competed successfully at the international level for nearly three decades, bringing home top prizes from top classes. She has competed at two FEI World Cup Finals and was on the US Equestrian Nations Cup Team in 2019. Jenni's career focus remains on opportunities to qualify and ride for the US Equestrian Team. ◆

www.teammcallister.com

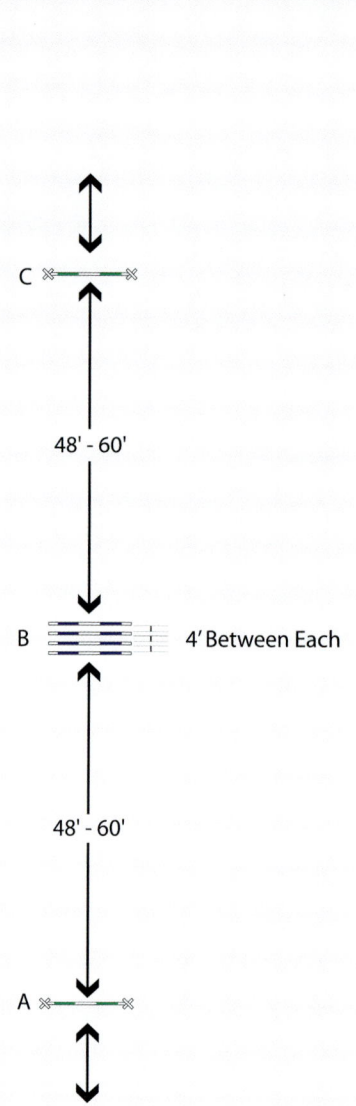

reason. Not only is it versatile in that you can adjust the distances to fit almost any arena or riding space, it is also suitable for most horse-and-rider combinations. The adaptations are endless, it's easy to set up and tear down or can be left in your arena.

The idea behind this exercise is to help learn the balance needed between the leg and hand for your horse to remain in balance throughout a series of transitions and obstacles. To be successful, your horse needs to be balanced on your aids, and riders need to be precise in their application of the aids. This exercise is aimed to get a quality trot over the trot poles that engages his back and energy in the same way you need to jump an oxer on course.

/ HOW

When you're warming up, start by just trotting through the exercise with Cavalletti A and C on the lowest height. Depending on the training level of yourself and your horse, you can even start by walking through everything a few times before picking up the trot. Regardless of how you start, do not continue until your horse is comfortably trotting everything.

The next step is to pick up your canter and head toward your first cavalletti (Cavalletti A or C). Again, depending on your level, this cavalletti can be anywhere from another ground pole to its full height.

Your goal from the very beginning is to canter in, transition to the trot for the ground poles, and then pick up your canter for the final cavalletti. For example, you could canter in over

GRID PRO QUO / *Margaret Rizzo McKelvy* /

Cavalletti A, transition to the trot before Ground Poles B, trot through Ground Poles B, pick up your canter, and canter over Cavalletti C. Or you can do the exercise in reverse.

For your downward transition, you will need to shorten your canter stride before you trot to help your horse stay balanced through the transition. Remember to ride from leg to hand and remain forward-thinking through this downward transition.

Your ability to have a prompt and balanced transition will dictate whether you're able to soften your aids before Ground Poles B, which is always the goal. You never want to tackle an obstacle, whether it's poles on the ground or a 1.40-meter oxer, with a horse that is against your aids.

After your ground poles you want to aim to pick up a balanced canter to finish over your final cavalletti. It's important your horse is responsive to your aids for both the upward and downward transitions, so be sure to test this out in your warm-up before you even start over the cavalletti.

Don't be stressed if you make a mess of the exercise at first. It's not uncommon to struggle while making your transitions, and this is why using cavalletti and ground poles is so beneficial here. You can repeat this exercise quite a lot without pounding on your horse's legs.

When that becomes too easy, you can start changing things up by introducing a variety of options:

1. *Canter in on one lead, trot, and finish on the other lead.*

2. *Gallop in to your first cavalletti.*

3. *Change where you make your transitions, challenging yourself to make them closer and closer to the ground poles.*

4. *Change the placement of the cavalletti.*

5. *Move the cavalletti to create a bending line.*

Personally, I don't think there's a wrong way to do this exercise. It teaches you what you need to work on, so be sure to be honest with yourself and be self-reflective as you work your way through it. ◆

THE EXERCISES

EXPERT EXERCISE

Cavalletti and Traditional Gymnastic

Margaret McKelvy

of Mythic Landing Enterprises in Mount Airy, Maryland

▽ About the expert:

Margaret McKelvy boasts an extensive career in competitive equestrian sports with a focus on eventing. She has been lucky to ride with a number of accomplished instructors and believes that this has helped develop her into a well-rounded horsewoman. When she is not on horseback, she manages her own public relations, event planning, and business development service with a team of professional consultants. She and her husband reside in the Washington, DC, area. ◆

This is a low-impact exercise that works to improve your horse's shape over jumps, while also giving the rider time to work on her own position. This is a great exercise to utilize when coming back into work, or when your horse needs a tune-up between shows.

/ MATERIALS NEEDED

- 3 ground poles or cavalletti
- 6 jump poles
- 2 sets of standards

/ SETUP

- This exercise doesn't require a lot of space but does require a fair number of poles and cavalletti.

- If you don't have cavalletti, you can easily substitute additional ground poles.

GRID PRO QUO / *Margaret Rizzo McKelvy* /

/ 132

/ WHY

While I most often jump in lessons, I do jump on my own from time to time, and whenever I do, I take a moment to think about what I want to accomplish during that jump school. I like this particular exercise because it's a nice combination of footwork, strength work, and coursework. As an amateur rider with one horse, I do not want to unnecessarily pound on my horse's legs. But I also need to make sure I practice enough to be prepared for my competitions. I've found this exercise checks all the boxes.

This particular exercise is a combination of things I've learned from both of my regular instructors, Kelley Williams and Stephen Bradley. The bounces come from Stephen's lessons and the cross-rail/verticals come from Kelley's lessons.

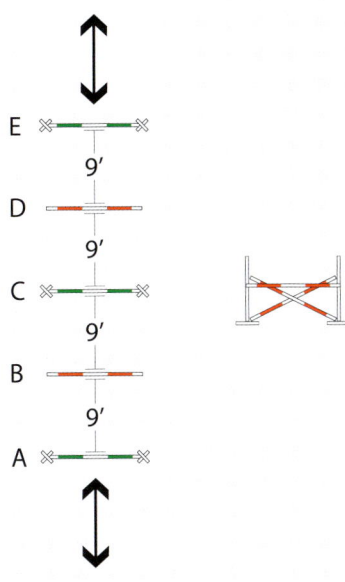

/ HOW

Before you start jumping, make sure you test all your buttons. Lengthen and shorten your horse's stride, and move your horse from side to side. Spend some time moving your horse's body around so that he is loose and relaxed through his body and mind, and you know that your aids are working as intended. Also spend a little time really focusing on the connection in the bridle.

Regardless of your level, start with all your jump poles on the ground and your cavalletti on the lowest height. If your horse is very green, walk him through all the elements a few times before picking up the trot and trotting him through. Don't be in a rush to start jumping.

Remember you're trying to be efficient in your jumping, so the more time you spend working over the ground poles, the more likely you'll be to breeze through the jumping portion. Be picky about your connection and your horse's response to your aids. If your horse isn't listening to your leg aid over trot poles, the issue is likely to only get worse once you have jumps.

If you're trying to save your horse's legs, finish your warm-up by trotting through your poles, and then have a prompt upward canter transition and go over a single cavalletti or ground pole that you have randomly placed elsewhere in the arena.

THE EXERCISES

Once you're ready to start jumping, you can begin in a few different ways, depending on your horse's level of training. This exercise is designed to be entered at a trot and exited at a canter. The placement of Jumps B and D in relation to your cavalletti will help your horse establish an elastic and balanced canter with a smooth and consistent stride length. For greener horses, leave everything on the ground, and build a small cross-rail as Jump B. If your horse is more experienced, you can start with two small cross-rails as Jumps B and D. After a time or two through, go ahead and add in your vertical rail to complete your cross-rail/vertical construction at Jumps B and D, as illustrated in the diagram.

Since you spent so much time on your warm-up, you may be able to build up your jumps rather quickly. Try to start with everything set slightly below your competition height, before gradually raising the obstacles.

Now you have a choice of what to do with your cross-rail/vertical jump construction (Jumps B and D). When your horse struggles with straightness, leave the vertical rail small and raise up your cross-rails to encourage your horse to find the center. But also think about why your horse may be crooked. Every horse (just like every person) has his own quirks or areas of soreness and will inevitably travel a little crookedly to compensate. Some horses also use crookedness as an expression of evasion or disobedience. Depending on your horse, he may be quite adamant about being crooked. As his rider, you must try to determine the reason for that crookedness—disobedience versus soreness. So, as you go through this exercise, be aware of your straightness and you'll be surprised by how much it affects your horse's rhythm and regulation.

If you want to make this more of a strength-building exercise for your horse, leave your cross-rail low and raise up your vertical rail in Jumps B and D. And if you have a horse that is slow with his hind end, play around with raising Cavalletti A, C, and E slightly—no more than 6 to 8 inches—to encourage your horse to keep thinking about his hind legs. If you choose either of these options, be mindful that the distances in this gymnastic make it a workout, so be kind to your horse. When you feel him getting tired, give him a break.

As a rider, your only job through this trot gymnastic is to stay tall and support your horse through the exercise with your leg. You will quickly find that the exercise will do all the work, so you just need to get your horse there and let the gymnastic do the rest.

GRID PRO QUO / Margaret Rizzo McKelvy /

If your horse is just coming back into jumping work, or it's the middle of winter and your next competition is months away, you can give him a pat after working through the trot gymnastic and go for a hack. But if you're preparing for a competition, add in some coursework exercises of your choosing.

Just remember that while this trot gymnastic does a lot to help you, you will have to start working harder when you add in coursework. Your trot gymnastic, when done well, will leave you with a lovely uphill canter perfect for jumping a course. The challenge is keeping this canter as you work through your course.

The nice part about this setup is that if your canter starts to get flat or your horse starts to wiggle, you can simply come back to the trot and reset your canter through the trot gymnastic (which should be reset to a lower height). ◆

EXPERT

Heather Parish

of Spring Meadow Farm in Hugo, Minnesota

▽ **About the expert:**

A lifelong horsewoman, Heather Parish is the head trainer at Spring Meadow Farm in Minnesota. Her knowledge and firsthand experience make her well-respected within the horse community. She combines her horse expertise with lessons she's learned as an elementary school teacher to bring out the best in her students. ◆

www.springmeadowfarm-mn.com

EXERCISE

Cavalletti and Coursework

This exercise is a great combination of footwork and coursework that can be practiced throughout the year. It doesn't require a lot of space or materials and can prove useful for horses and riders of all levels.

/ MATERIALS NEEDED

- 4 cavalletti
- 1 jump pole
- 1 set of standards

/ SETUP

- Set up your jump first in the center of your arena.

- Next set up your two sets of cavalletti, leaving them set to the lowest height.

- The distances between the exercises can vary depending on the size of your arena, but

GRID PRO QUO / Margaret Rizzo McKelvy /

in an ideal world you'll have space to make a 20-meter circle around your cavalletti.

/ WHY

One of the main reasons I like this exercise is because it doesn't require a lot of space or a lot of materials to set it up. It's also something that can be left in your arena, as you can easily work around everything when flatting your horses. I like that it is a nice combination of footwork exercises and coursework exercises. It helps horses to learn how to balance and then carry that balance on into their coursework.

For the rider, it really teaches you to use your space and use it well. I find that in small spaces my students are tempted to cut their turns, which inevitably makes everything more difficult. The simple setup of the cavalletti combined with the single jump really help riders be able to focus on their track and not worry about a complicated course.

/ HOW

First, when setting up your cavalletti, you should have 9 to 10 feet in the middle. Don't be afraid to adjust that distance based on your horse's natural way of going.

To start, create a circle over one set of cavalletti, and trot the cavalletti, working on putting one or two steps between them. Try to alternate between one and two steps by asking your horse to go more forward or to collect on the circle, and by varying your line. You can get your two steps easily by staying out on your circle where

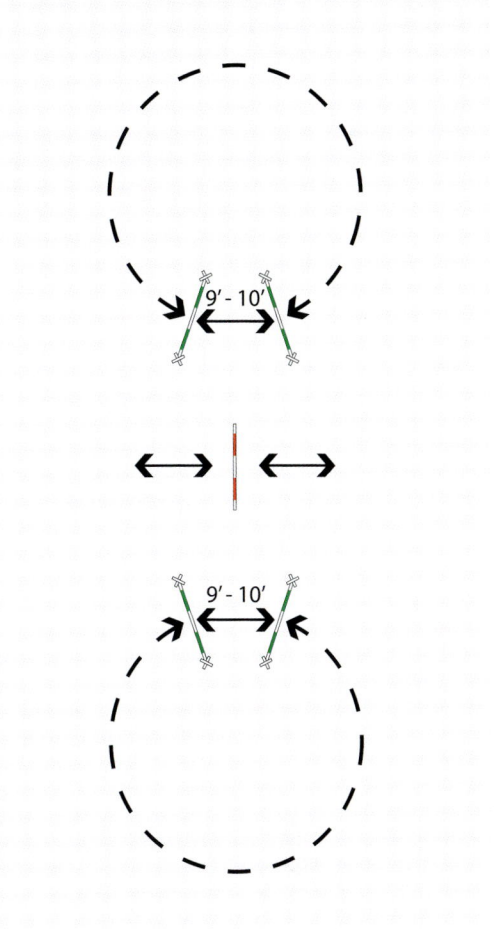

there is more space between the cavalletti, and your one step is made easier by staying in on your circle. The goal is to be able to go from one to two steps, then back to one step seamlessly and easily.

Alternate between the two sets of cavalletti by working over two at one end of the arena and then going down the long side to work in a circle over the other set of cavalletti.

THE EXERCISES

Once you are working over both sets of cavalletti in balance and in rhythm, it's time raise your cavalletti to their top height and pick up your canter. This time your only striding option is to bounce the cavalletti.

To challenge yourself, work on collecting and lengthening down the long side between your circles.

Then add in your center jump, which can be anything you want it to be, whether a vertical, oxer, or simply a pile of poles on the ground. Work your horse over this center jump in another circle, then use your cavalletti bounces to regroup and rebalance. Be sure to change directions over this center jump so you can work on both leads, and recognize where you might need to work more.

As an added challenge, count the number of steps on each of your circles. This will help you connect the feeling of the canter with the number of strides between fences. For example, if you had a nice, balanced trip through the cavalletti with 15 steps around the circle, but then fumbled through it when you only had 13 steps, you know that the 13 steps were probably too strung out. By counting, you learn how to find the right canter for the right exercise. ◆

EXERCISE

Coursework

EXPERT

Richard Picken

of Four Schools Farm in Paris, Kentucky

▽ **About the expert:**

This is a great exercise for solidifying two important riding concepts: inside leg to outside rein, and riding from leg to hand. The variety of jumps and exercises also allow for this exercise to be adaptable for horses and riders of all levels.

/ MATERIALS NEEDED

- 4 ground poles
- 4 cavalletti
- 12 jump poles
- 7 sets of standards

/ SETUP

- While this exercise does take a lot of space to set up fully, it is possible to still experience the benefits of it if you're only able to set up parts of it. Just get creative and do the elements that you can.

A native of the United Kingdom, Richard Picken grew up in a show jumping family. When he turned 16, he left home to work in Holland and Canada for nearly three decades, where he rode with Graham Fletcher, Stal Hendrix, George Morris, and Ian Millar. He coaches elite athletes and young riders, and fills his days traveling for clinics, coaching at home, or warming up riders at major competitions around the United States and overseas. ◆

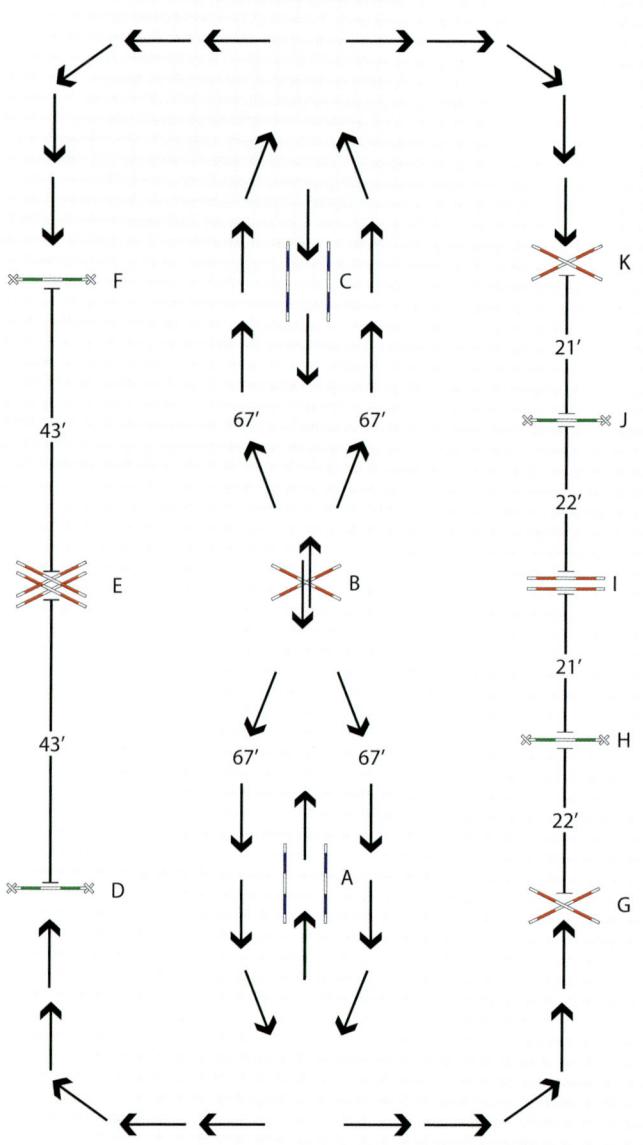

/ WHY

Those who have been to my clinics are probably familiar with the centerline exercise featured here. It is a staple of my program for several reasons, the main one being that it is suitable for horses and riders of all levels. While the exercise is fairly basic on paper, it is quite effective in teaching the rider about two important concepts: inside leg to outside rein and using your leg before your hand.

As you land off the centerline cross-rail (Jump B) and leg-yield to either side of the poles on the ground (Ground Poles A or C), you will help solidify teaching your horse to move off your leg, specifically your inside leg. The poles on the ground are a great visual for how reactive your horse is, or isn't, to your leg. Once you are easily able to move your horse off your inside leg, you can remember that feeling when you come to a corner so your horse does

GRID PRO QUO / *Margaret Rizzo McKelvy* /

not fall in. The same concept applies when you're riding a bending line of multiple fences.

When teaching, I often see riders try to use their reins to move their horse to either side of the poles on the ground. It won't take more than a time or two through the exercise for the riders to realize that they need to put their leg on to initiate their horse moving over. Since Jump B is simply a cross-rail, you can repeat this exercise over and over until you get it right.

The remaining exercises in the diagram give riders plenty to do to have a complete jump school. You'll quickly notice that the distances aren't always perfect, and they are meant to be adjusted by a foot or so here and there. Not all course designers are going to set up the perfect distance every time. So it's best to practice slightly odd distances in your everyday life so you learn to adjust the horse's stride throughout your courses.

Another reason why I love this setup is that it teaches riders (and horses) that it's not the actual distance that's important. It's how the horse is jumping the jumps. So even if you spent your first day or two with this exercise with all the poles on the ground, you can work with your horse to create an adjustable canter that can jump any jump from any distance.

/ HOW

Before you start jumping, make sure that you can seamlessly move your horse forward and back, and laterally from side to side. By seamlessly, I mean that I want to see the horse is accepting and responsive to the rider's aids.

Once you're confident you're working together as a team, start with Exercise 1, but take Jump E out so there are just Cavalletti D and F on the ends. As you go through Cavalletti D and F, count your strides.

PRO TIPS

I often have people question why the distances are just slightly different between jumps G, H, I, J, and K in Exercise 2, and my reason is quite simple: while it's only a foot, it's enough to make a difference. Keep in mind that this particular exercise is a little easier when you approach it from the 22-foot distance, so I do like to start with that approach. As I mentioned earlier, I like to mix things up a bit so that the horse and rider get used to thinking throughout their course. The goal is to be a proactive rider, not just a reactive rider.

From here, add and take out strides between the cavalletti to work on adjustability. Depending on your level, you should be able to add or take out one to four strides.

As soon as your horse is able to seamlessly play with the striding in both directions between the cavalletti, add in the cross-rail/oxer (Jump E) and build it up until it's at an appropriate level for your horse and yourself. Keep in mind that this is a cross-rail oxer, which helps you stay visually centered and encourages the horse to be a bit more tidy with his front end.

From here you can move to Exercise 2, and once again start by going through it a few times with Jump G, I, and K taken out and just Cavalletti H and J in place before adding in the jumps.

Once your horse is straight and adjustable in relation to your riding level, move on to Exercise 3. Again, simplify the exercise to start, putting the centerline cross-rail (Jump B) poles down on the ground. Exercises 1 and 2 focus on longitudinal adjustability, and Exercise 3 focuses on latitudinal adjustability. As discussed earlier, the idea is to leg-yield to either side of the poles on the ground. As the jump gets bigger, you need to concentrate on staying tall in the saddle, so that when you land you are ready to start your leg-yield.

I find that the biggest problem in course riding is riders cutting their corners. The goal of this entire jump sequence is to help with this common issue. So once you have mastered each exercise individually, put together small courses utilizing different aspects of the exercise's setup.

Regardless of the size of your jumping arena or your course, you should always work on staying on the rail between the exercises. If you are still struggling with your horse falling in on turns, try taking one more stride before turning to the next jump.

While advanced riders can move through all three exercises in one jump school, I often recommend riders leaving this exercise set up in their arena for a week or two and gradually work their way through it. If you have a smaller arena, put Exercise 3 across the diagonal, and the other distances can be adapted to fit into your space. And keep in mind that different horses need different things, so don't be afraid to adapt as needed. ◆

GRID PRO QUO / Margaret Rizzo McKelvy /

EXERCISE

Coursework and Turning

EXPERT

Caroline Powell

of Caroline Powell Eventing in Suffolk, East Anglia

This exercise is a good way to test your skills as a rider. The difficulty level can be easily matched to any horse-and-rider combination, making this a versatile exercise to leave set up in your arena.

/ MATERIALS NEEDED

- 4 jump poles
- 4 sets of standards

/ SETUP

- The distances here can be adjusted to fit your space, and you can set this up on either end of your arena or in the center.

- If you want to increase the difficulty, this can be set up in a field to include a little terrain.

▽ **About the expert:**

A New Zealand native, Caroline Powell has based herself in England for much of her professional career. She has represented her home country in two Olympics and two World Equestrian Games, winning an Olympic team bronze medal in 2012 and a World Equestrian Games team bronze medal in 2010. She won the Burghley Horse Trials in 2010 with her longtime partner Lenamore. ◆

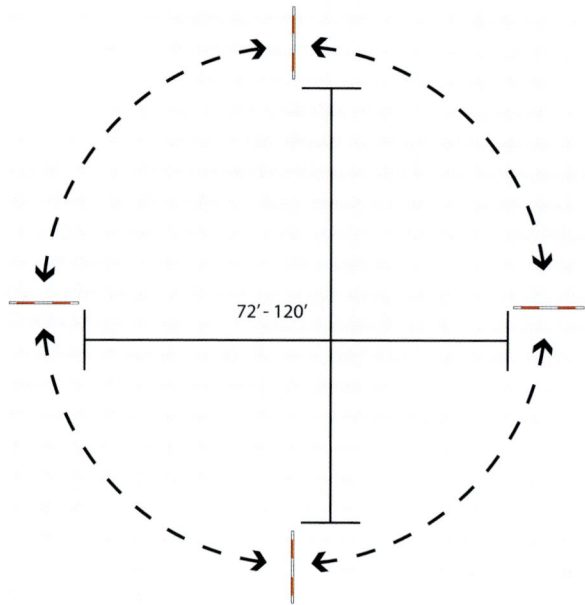

/ WHY

This is my favorite jumping exercise for horses and riders of all levels. It's quite simple on paper, but I've found that it helps to cure a lot of problems.

In my opinion, if you cannot canter around this exercise, there is no way you can have the control of speed, impulsion, shoulder, and line needed to successfully jump a course, regardless of whether you're out on cross-country or in the arena.

/ HOW

Before you get started, you need to remember four key points:

1. *The control of the canter is most important for all jumping phases.*

2. *The ability to guide and direct the canter is next.*

3. *Being able to control turns allows for speed and ultimately your ability to compete.*

4. *Canter control allows for an awareness of where you are in relationship to the fence.*

Depending on your level of competition, you can start with these as poles on the ground that you walk over. There's a saying that you need to walk before you run, and in this case, you should be able to walk before you canter!

GRID PRO QUO / *Margaret Rizzo McKelvy* /

At a walk you will be able to feel which way the horse loses his straightness and make the necessary corrections. Once you have complete control of your horse's speed, impulsion, shoulder, and line at the walk, then move on to the trot. And then the canter. Try counting strides as you go around the circle. The number of strides may vary between poles as you're getting started. However, the end goal is to consistently have the same number of strides between each set. This number is likely to vary depending on the distances you have set up, as well as your personal horse's stride length and level of training.

The key to mastering this exercise is to be patient and persistent in your pursuit of perfection. But also remember that what is perfect for an inexperienced four-year-old is going to look very different from what is perfect for a 14-year-old campaigner. Be realistic in your expectations, but persistent in your efforts to improve. ◆

EXPERT EXERCISE

Traditional Gymnastic

Valerie Pride

of Blue Clover Eventing in West River, Maryland

▽ About the expert:

Based out of the world-class Sudley Farm in West River, Maryland, Valerie Pride (née Vizcarrondo) stays busy as an active competitor, trainer, agent, clinician, and judge. She has competed through the CCI5* level of eventing and holds her FEI Level 2 license, which allows her to officiate through the four-star level. While Valerie loves the thrill of competing, she finds great pleasure in working with students and horses on a daily basis. Rest assured that anything and everything she does is accomplished with an abundance of enthusiasm and obsessive attention to detail! ◆

www.bluecloverEventing.com

This is a great exercise to work on your horse's adjustability and your own position over fences. There are a few variations that you can do to make the exercise user-friendly for horses and riders of all levels.

/ MATERIALS NEEDED

- 2 ground poles (optional)
- 12 jump poles
- 12 sets of standards

/ SETUP

- You have the option of setting these two exercises up separately or adjusting it as you go.

- For Exercise 1, if you want to make this a trot grid, your first bounce should be 10 feet apart and your second bounce 11 feet apart. If want a canter grid, your bounces should be 11 feet and 12 feet apart.

GRID PRO QUO / *Margaret Rizzo McKelvy* /

- You can start with all the jumps in place at a low height.

/ WHY

This is one of my favorite grids for all types of horses and riders because in just several fences, both horse and rider have to be masters at extremely different positions and shapes. Yet because of the distances and setup, the adjustability happens in a positive, user-friendly way.

Over these double bounces (Jumps A, B, and C) it is important that you stay tall, yet go with your horse, maintaining contact and support. It also teaches how to use your elbows and land over your knees quickly or in rapid succession. The hogsback (Jump D) is the strength-building part of this exercise because you must remain off your horse's back for the entire fence, which feels quite different, and exaggerated after the double bounces. The three strides between the bounces and hogsback give you plenty of time to adjust your position.

I also like the three-stride distance because it really helps you (and horse) be able to start to see your distances to the fences. If you think about it, most riders count down to their fences, "Three, two, one." With the three strides being right there for this grid, it helps you get the feeling of what the last three strides before a fence should be like—rhythmic, even, and steady.

For the horse, this grid is great because it makes him do all his jumping shapes in one exercise. First, you teach your horse to organize, balance, rock back, and more or less compress his stride over the bounces. Then you add the hogsback, and the key is to make it quite wide. This makes your compressed and organized horse then expand, lengthen, have a proper bascule, and learn how to finish his jump behind.

As any trainer will tell you, adjustability is one of the best tools you can teach your horse when it comes to competing. You'll find that just as you're teaching your horse adjustability, you as a rider will also learn to adjust more quickly and effectively to get through the exercise well.

I originally learned these grids in a lesson with the great Jimmy Wofford. I have since adapted them slightly to fit into my ring and work for my students. I typically use them for horse-and-rider combinations showing at 3 feet and higher. But by using one bounce instead of the double bounce, and making the hogsback into a simple ascending oxer, you can use this grid for lower levels as well.

THE EXERCISES

/ HOW

Regardless of your level, you always want to start small. I start out with everything set up at a height that is easy for your level of riding—whether this is 18 inches or 3 feet is up to you.

To help make the warm-up a bit smoother, you can put a placing rail 9 feet out on either side of Jump A. Start by trotting a few times over Jump A, and when that is going well, move on to cantering Jump A. As you're warming up, be sure to change directions often and approach the jump from both leads.

Once you and your horse are warmed up, add in Jump B to make up your first bounce. Be sure to have ground lines on either side of all your jumps. This will make the exercise look a bit serious, giving most horses a reason to give it some respect, versus just dashing through it or being lazy.

As you approach your first bounce, nothing should change in your canter. You should keep the nice quiet canter (or trot) that you had going over your warm-up vertical, and you should continue to change directions often.

One mistake that I often see with riders during bounce exercises is that they get too far ahead of the motion. So if you're repeating one thing in your head as you approach the first bounce, it should be, "Heels down, shoulders up. Heels down, shoulders up." Seems simple, right? But if there is any exercise that requires you to stay tall and balanced, it is these double bounces! So repeat the single bounce until it goes smoothly.

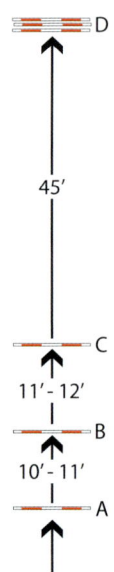

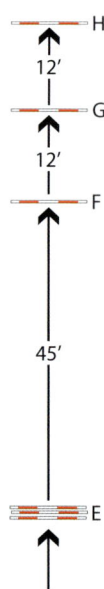

GRID PRO QUO / Margaret Rizzo McKelvy /

After you've gone through the single bounce from both directions, you can go ahead and add in Jump C to complete your second bounce.

At this point, I like to change the heights of the verticals so that they are all different heights. This helps the horses, especially the younger ones, read the exercise. Once you've gone through the double bounces well, you can do one of two things depending on your horse. If your horse is getting through the bounces, but not really using himself, you can raise the jumps to a height that gets his attention. Once he is really rocking back in front of Jump A and staying quick with his front end throughout, you can move on.

On the other hand, if your horse was trying hard through the bounces, you can move on and add in the hogsback (Jump D). Although, for the first time or two through, just use the first two sets of standards for an ascending oxer.

Remember that the key to this exercise is to get three even, rhythmic strides between your bounces and Jump D. The 45 feet is the perfect distance for this for 95 percent of horses. But if your horse is struggling with the distance for any reason, go ahead and adjust it to make it easier on him.

As a rider, this exercise should help you gain confidence in riding to an oxer. This exercise also helps you figure out the right amount of leg to put on and helps you develop your eye, since the distance is an easy three strides away.

After a time or two over Jump D as an ascending oxer, go ahead and add the back rail to complete your hogsback. You should be prepared for your horse to be a little surprised by the back rail the first or second time as he adjusts to the added effort needed to form a proper bascule over the hogsback. Once you're comfortable with this, you can adjust the height of the hogsback to whatever height suits your needs.

For more experienced horses, you can turn the exercise around so that they have to jump the hogsback first, and then balance over the bounces, as illustrated in Exercise 2. This brings with it a whole new set of challenges, so for the first time or two through, lower the fences back to something you and your horse will consider easy. This is particularly great for horses who rush or get strong after the oxers.

If at any point you run into problems, don't be afraid to break down the exercise to help restore your horse's confidence. If this means making the bounce verticals into small cross-rails, then go ahead and do it. Above all things your horse needs to be straight and forward and confident. So if you need to put the rails on the ground for a time or two, go ahead and do that, then carefully build the exercise back up. ◆

THE EXERCISES

EXPERT EXERCISE

Cavalletti and Traditional Gymnastic

Waylon Roberts

of JWR Sporthorses in Opelika, Alabama

▽ About the expert:

Waylon Roberts has been representing Canada in international competition since the age of 14, when he attended the 2002 FEI Children's Final for show jumping in Brazil. Since then, he has ridden at the North American Junior and Young Riders Championships and the Pan American Games. He has trained with some of the world's top riders and competed at some of the world's most prestigious events, including the Kentucky CCI5* on several occasions. When not competing, Waylon can be found teaching and training at his new home base in Alabama. ◆

www.jwrsporthorses.com

These exercises are all about footwork for your horse and position strengthening for the rider. The jumps can be anything from poles on the ground on up, making these suitable for all riders.

/ MATERIALS NEEDED

- 6 cavalletti
- 11 jump poles
- 7 sets of standards

/ SETUP

- When set up fully, these exercises do require a large arena. However, if you are short on space you can split each exercise in half and get creative.

- To get started put all the cavalletti and jump poles on the ground.

GRID PRO QUO / Margaret Rizzo McKelvy /

/ WHY

These are my favorite jumping exercises for the off season. Before getting caught up in the rush to get ready for your next competition, it's great to spend a little time working on footwork exercises for your horse and position exercises for yourself. Without the pressure of competing, it's the perfect time to take a breath and really focus on the details.

In addition to helping horses with their footwork, this is great for working on your horse's suppleness and core strength while jumping. It's not uncommon for horses to get stiff and flat while on course, so it's important to spend the time to teach them how to effectively use their bodies to create a better jump. For the rider to be successful, she must be aware of the effect of her aids throughout a series of jumps. And since the jumps stay relatively small throughout these exercises, there's no harm in repeating them over and over until you get them right. Like most gymnastic exercises, it's usually quite clear when you get it right, so while it's always helpful to have a good set of eyes on the ground, it's possible to work through these on your own if you stay focused and honest with yourself about your mistakes.

The other thing that these exercises are good for is teaching riders to keep their leg on and follow the horse's jump with both their hand and their seat. Because, as I like to say, jumping without leg or a forgiving contact is like finding a black cat in a dark room with the cat door open.

/ HOW

Before you even start jumping, it's important to make sure your horse is properly warmed up on the flat. No amount of jumping exercises will improve a poorly started or nervous horse, so you have to be sure that you have taught your horse well on the flat and your horse knows about contact and leg. This exercise will certainly help further your training, but you must make sure you have the basics down before starting.

Once you are ready to start jumping, you should begin with Cavalletti A or C in Exercise 1 on a 15-meter circle. At first, all cavalletti should be on the ground, and you should trot through them a time or two in each direction to show your horse where he is going. If you have a young or inexperienced horse, you can always walk through them first.

THE EXERCISES

EXERCISE 1

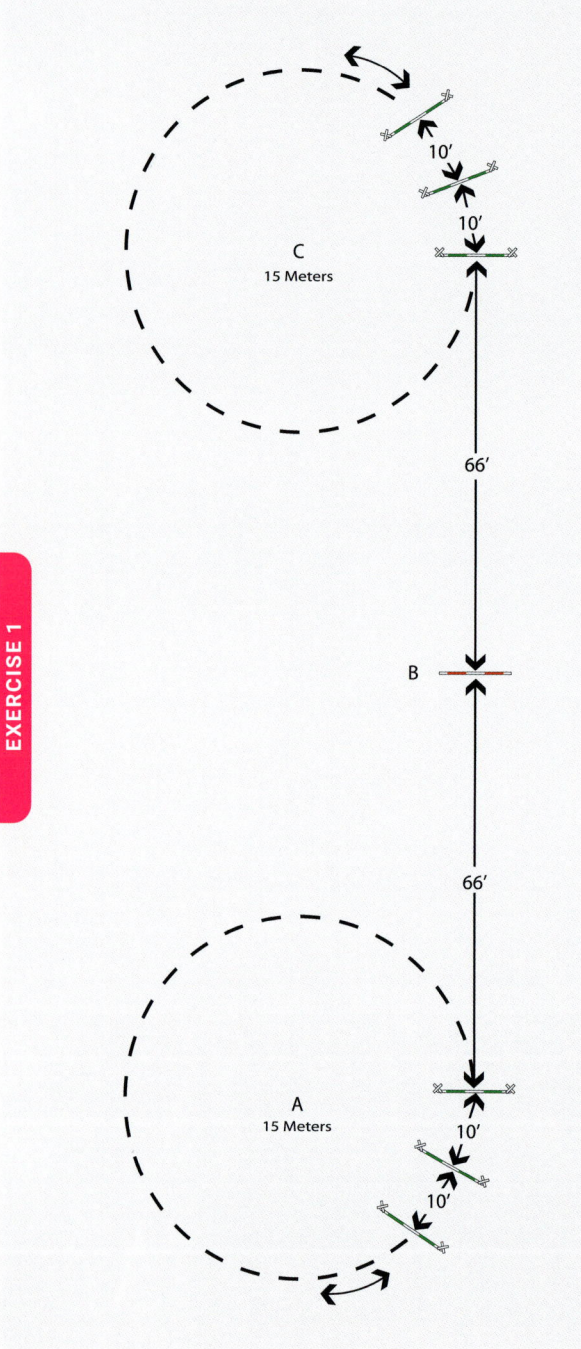

Regardless of the level of your horse, the goal is to introduce these cavalletti in a stress-free way. A tense horse will have a harder time learning and working through his body than a relaxed horse. So relaxation is always the goal.

Once you are confidently and quietly trotting through one set of the cavalletti, you can begin cantering through them, still on that 15-meter circle. You should then begin raising the cavalletti height based on your horse's experience. For most of my young horses, I will stick to the lowest height with the cavalletti on the ground. My more advanced horses will quickly progress to the cavalletti at their top height.

Regardless of the height of the cavalletti or where you are in the warm-up stage, you need to always be aware of your inside aids and use your inside leg to help keep the horse from leading with the inside shoulder through the curve. I like to alternate which set of cavalletti (A or C) I'm working through as I warm up, which allows my horse to see everything in Exercise 1 while it is still easy.

I find this a good exercise to help with rushing horses, as it's hard for them to cleanly make their way through the exercise if they do not take their time. It's also the first part of this series that really helps to teach

GRID PRO QUO / *Margaret Rizzo McKelvy* /

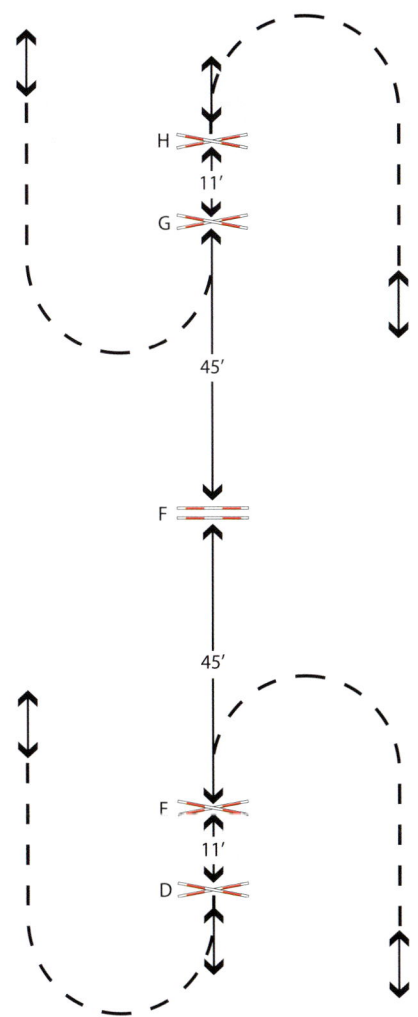

EXERCISE 2

the rider to follow her horse's jump with both her hand and her seat.

The next part of Exercise 1 starts with one set of cavalletti but incorporates a small vertical (Jump B) in the center. The distance between the cavalletti and Jump B can be adjusted according to the size of the arena, however I most like it set at 66 feet, so the horses have a quiet five strides between Jump B and each set of cavalletti.

Repeat riding from one set of cavalletti to the other, over Jump B, on both reins until the striding is even and quiet. For riders who are struggling to see their distance, I like them to count their strides out loud. Not only does this help them be more aware of their striding, but it also keeps them breathing! I do like to keep Jump B fairly low for the level, until the horse can stay balanced on an even stride without getting strung out. This portion of the exercise teaches the horse and rider rhythm, patience, and straightness.

If this has been accomplished without much fuss, the pair can move on to Exercise 2. To start here, you can canter each cross-rail bounce (Jumps E and D, or Jumps G and H) off a long approach to the centerline, and depart from each jump with a rollback turn away from the centerline. So if you are on the left lead, you canter

THE EXERCISES

down the long side of the arena and turn down the centerline to have a long approach to the cross-rail bounce closest to the other end of the arena. Upon landing, you make a rollback turn to the right, away from the centerline. This rollback not only helps to create a lead change, but it also helps the rider learn how to switch the inside legs over the jump to show the horse a correlation between the leg, the lead change, and the bounce.

This can be a little intense for some horses, so be sure to keep the cross-rails low until they have their confidence in the exercise. And be sure to rest and reward your horse often. Again, since the jumps are small, it's fine to repeat as needed, but you should never repeat until exhaustion.

From here the pair are ready to include the oxer (Jump F). Again, if you want to start on the right lead, you will jump your first bounce (Jumps D and E), stay straight for three strides to the oxer (Jump F), and then another straight three strides to the second bounce (Jumps G and H). The horse should hold his lead throughout the exercise and the rider must now work to keep the horse straight.

Again, you are looking to improve the horse's rhythm, straightness, and patience to and away from a fence. Always keep the jumps low until the horse and you are confident, then you can play around with the height to challenge yourself. ◆

EXERCISE

Traditional Gymnastic

EXPERT

Jenn Schuessler

of Jenn Simmons Eventing in Delaplane, Virginia

These are great exercises for riders to work through if they are thinking about moving up a level. They are also super for instilling confidence in horses that may need a little boost.

/ MATERIALS NEEDED

- 6 ground poles
- 14 jump poles
- 14 sets of standards

/ SETUP

- It is good to have a jump crew help with setup, as there are a lot of poles and jumps.

- While the exercises look complicated, they are not very long, so you can typically set this up in most arenas.

▽ **About the expert:**

Advanced-Level rider Jenn Schuessler (née Simmons) has been an active member of the eventing community for more than 20 years. After being a working student, then barn manager for eventing legend Jimmy Wofford, Jenn struck out on her own. After a successful career in the horse world, Jenn moved onto a career in corporate America. While still a horse professional, she was happy to work with anybody interested in riding better, whether fox hunter, new event rider, young rider, or more experienced riders. Jenn feels that having patience and building confidence is the best approach to both horse and rider. ◆

- You can get creative with your Ground Poles F, L, and R, and use anything from two rails put together to a flower box.

/ WHY

These are my favorite exercises for horses and riders looking to move up a level, whether from cross-rails to 2 feet 6 inches, or 3 feet 9 inches to 4 feet. It's a great way to give horses confidence in themselves. When horses jump with the most confidence, they trust in their ability to let go in their bodies, which means they soften their jump.

When a horse is tense, nervous, spooky, or not sure of something, he tends to be very tight in his body, not just his brain, which can manifest in a variety of ways. The obvious ones are a runout or a stop, but he can also twist laterally, jump over his shoulder, or forget his hind end, which will all contribute to having rails come down on course. Another style flaw is when the horse lands too deep—or too close to the jump—which causes the distance to be too long to the next. Or he can land too far out, which can really get you into trouble, because you run out of room to the next fence.

The distances in these exercises are set to help boost your horse's confidence, so he learns to let go, relax, and use his body. I tell my students that bounces for their horse are like the tire-hopping exercises that football players do. It builds a lot of strength and dexterity. Here, the double bounces make him quick with his feet at the beginning of the exercises. They also act as a "placing rail" to the latter part of the exercises—whatever it is you are jumping out, whether a vertical, oxer, one stride, three stride, or in-and-out.

For the rider, you learn how to follow the motion. The bounces make it very clear, very quickly, whether you are out of balance or not. And since the jumps stay relatively low, you can go through several times and make the necessary adjustments.

I have been using variations of these exercises for years, but recently added landing rails at the suggestion of jumper rider Silvio Mazzoni, and they are great for both horse and rider. For the horse that "forgets" his hind end and drags through the rails, it will teach him to finish his jump behind. Or for the horse that jumps too far out, it's a great tool to help him improve his style.

For my horses, I find that I need to use two rails placed together for the landing rail in order for them to be respectful. I also sometimes use a low flower box—with or without flowers—against the rail to get their attention. You'd be surprised how much this can change the exercises! I also keep changing the "fillers" as I'm jumping. Maybe I'll start with a flower box at the pole leading into the exercise, only to move it to the landing rail later on. This is a great way to help other riders out by acting as jump crew for each other. You'll get a little extra exercise, learn a little something, and make it a safe situation for those schooling.

I often use these after a competition, as my horses tend to come back from competition feeling like they're Superman. This gets their focus, slows them down and gets them thinking about their bodies again. Jumping on bravado won't last very long, and our horses need to learn that they need to think about their job.

What I really love about these exercises is that they really set up both the horse and rider for success. Each piece of the exercises—ground poles, verticals, distances—are designed in a way that lead to the next and gives confidence to both horse and rider. It is the perfect, safe opportunity to raise the rails up to a height a little outside your comfort zone, without having to canter down to a large square oxer in the middle of the field. This is why I often use these for horses and riders getting ready to move up a level.

/ HOW

Depending on the level of horse and rider, you can start Exercise 1 in a few different ways. For confident 2-foot-9-inch pairs and above, you can put all the jumps in right away, just at very low heights. For less experienced pairs, you can start with all the rails on the ground and gradually put the jumps in one by one.

Whether you're starting with rails on the ground or starting with 2-foot verticals, repeat Exercise 1 at the current height until both horse and rider are going through it confidently. As an instructor and trainer, I make my students or horses repeat the exercise if there was any loss of rhythm or straightness. Once they get it right once, I want them to repeat it to make sure it wasn't a fluke! And if there is a loss of rhythm or straightness again, we'll continue until the exercise is completed well twice in a row. If this is the first time you do this exercise, and you don't make it past 2-foot verticals, that's okay! Just keep the exercise set up in your ring until you jump again.

If during your warm-up your horse starts to rush through, change things up a bit and jump the bounces going in the opposite direction (from Jump D to B) and halt in a straight line afterward. After doing this a few times, do the bounces to the vertical (Jump E) and halt again. Be sure you're not making a big deal about the halt. It should not be aggressive but instead a quiet, matter-of-fact halt. Once the horse stops, it's all praise! When your horse starts to get it, simply come back to a trot at the end, so your horse doesn't think it's a big deal. Both the horse and rider should be thinking after the jumps, not just saying, "Phew, I survived it!"

Be sure you're not giving your horse a reason to pull by checking your own position. The old saying, "Your horse cannot pull when he has nothing to pull against," is very true. Do not try to "hold the horse together" too much, which just causes him to rush more. The bounces make it very hard for a horse to rush, so let the exercise do the work.

Make your life easier by being really smart while schooling at home and change things up. Change directions often, and throw in a halt here and there. You can also use props around the arena to make things more interesting. This can be as simple as laying your jacket across one of the verticals, or adding a flower box in front of the final vertical.

On the flip side, if your horse is really lazy when you start out, simply drop your reins until you are close to the buckle and canter through the small verticals—or rails on the ground—until the horse is keeping his rhythm through the exercise. If you make a big deal about it, your horse might think that there's something to worry about. So I like to take the opposite approach, and show my horse that not only can he do this exercise with me, he should be able to do this exercise on his own.

When you work through Exercise 1 confidently a few times, the next step is to make the final vertical into an oxer (Jump K) as illustrated in Exercise 2. But be sure to lower your vertical (Jump E) back to your competition level before adding in a second rail for the oxer (Jump K). The change to the oxer is more of a *mental* challenge for the rider and a *physical* challenge for the horse. You will need to control any instinct to change your ride just because of the added back rail. Your horse will simply need to put some extra effort in to now jump across the width of the oxer without getting flat, which would most likely cause you to pull the rail. Remember all that time you spent jumping through the bounces and small verticals to create the right canter in Exercise 1? This is where it comes in handy!

The final piece to the puzzle is to move the oxer out to 45 feet beyond the bounces as illustrated in Exercise 3. This distance is typically

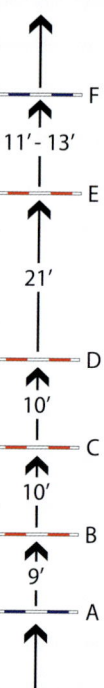

GRID PRO QUO / Margaret Rizzo McKelvy /

a snug three strides, but with the double bounce (Jumps N, O, and P) setting you up, it's a great distance to practice. Now the challenge is to maintain the canter that you've been fostering earlier in the jump school. If you've been doing your homework, you will quietly pop over the bounces and then canter down to your oxer. As you work through this exercise, you need to focus on keeping your eyes up and looking ahead, because everything happens so quickly that if you look down, you will often lose your position over the fences.

Don't be afraid to use this exercise to challenge yourself with bigger fences. As I said earlier, all the pieces are designed to set you up for success, so it's the perfect time to challenge your comfort zone a bit. As you jump through you want to keep your shoulders up, eyes up, and legs on your horse's sides. I'll often tell my students to think about keeping their shoulders

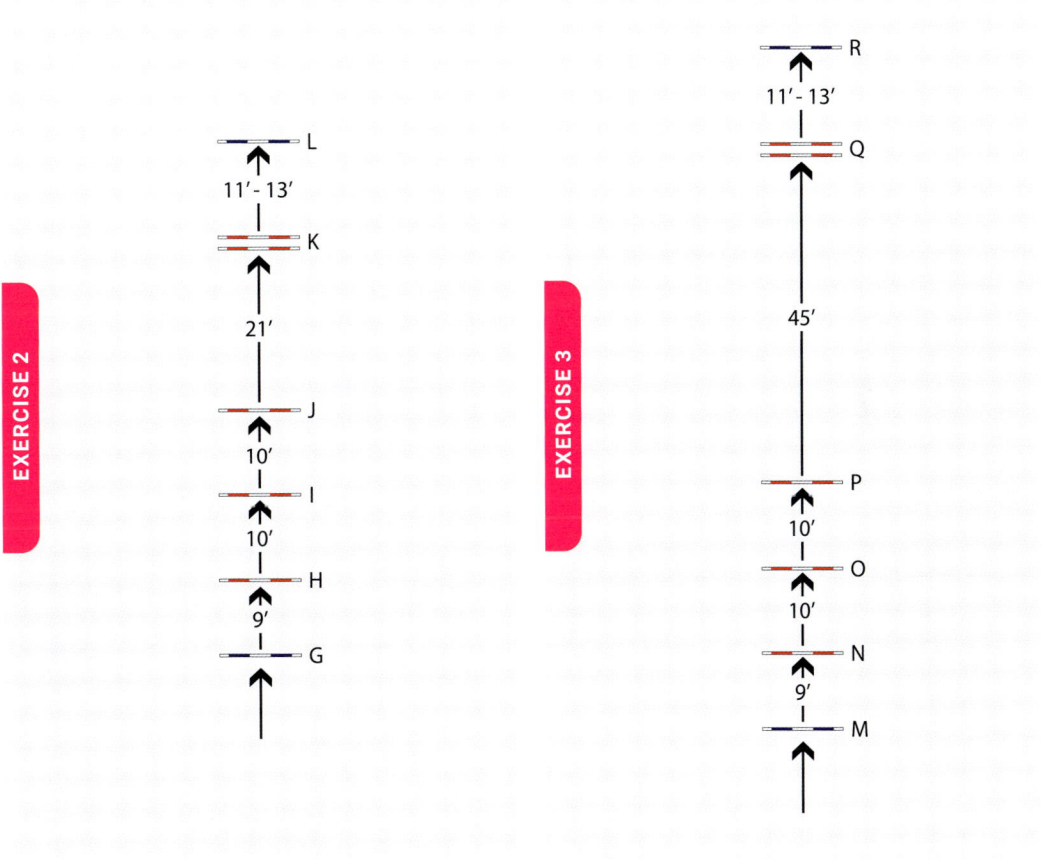

THE EXERCISES

behind their hips, which usually brings them into the correct position of their shoulders being above their hips. A lot of times, riders want to jump for their horses, so if my students are going to make a mistake, I would rather they be left behind than jump ahead of their horses.

At every stage, have a landing rail (Ground Pole F, L, or R) after your vertical (Jump E) or oxer (Jump K or Q). I don't have a set distance that I insist on using for this, instead I watch the horse jump through a few times then place it where it makes sense. Often, this is 11 feet away from the last jump (Jump E, K, or Q). As I mentioned before, the landing rail helps your horse learn to finish off his jump, and it helps the rider learn to keep riding. If a rider is having trouble focusing after the exercise, I set markers out throughout the ring and give them a "job" after the grid. This can be something as simple as circling around the cone in the corner, or as complicated as leg-yielding into the corner. I often do this with my training horses as well, because it teaches the horse the same work ethic (as well as being a good reminder for myself to keep riding!). ◆

EXERCISE

Coursework and Turning

EXPERT

Kim Severson

of Kim Severson Eventing in Charlottesville, Virginia

This is a great exercise for those that struggle with remaining effective throughout an entire course of jumps. While it appears simple on paper, there are infinite possibilities to make this as difficult, or as easy, as you need it to be.

/ MATERIALS NEEDED

- 7 jump poles
- 7 sets of standards
- 2 cones

/ SETUP

- The two oxers can be set along the quarterline of your jumping arena, with the single fences placed close to your centerline.

- While the distances here are what I prefer, they can be adjusted to fit within your space.

▽ **About the expert:**

A lifelong horsewoman, Kim Severson bases herself in Charlottesville, Virginia, at her own farm. She is probably best known for the storybook partnership with Winsome Adante ("Dan") that saw three wins at Kentucky CCI5*—in 2002, 2004, and 2006—plus a team gold medal at the 2002 World Equestrian Games in Spain, and culminating with an individual silver medal and team bronze medal at the 2004 Olympic Games in Greece. Known for her innate ability to transform an average horse into a top-quality competitor, Kim is also an experienced instructor who enjoys bringing the best out of her students. ◆

www.kimberlyseversoneventing.com

/ WHY

If you have been to one of my clinics, you have probably seen this exercise as it has become a favorite of mine, and I often have it set up in my arena at home. Two of the many reasons why I love this exercise are because not only is it easy for the clinic organizer to set up, but it is also an exercise that riders can take home with them and easily set up in their own arenas.

While there are only four jumps, there are infinite possibilities within the exercise, and the rider is able to tackle a variety of issues depending on what the individual horse needs to focus on. Additionally, as the skillset of the horse and rider increases, it is easy to increase the difficulty of the exercise.

Having taught for many years now, I have found that one of the biggest struggles for riders is to simply keep riding and keep being effective through an entire exercise. Whether it is at home or at a show, I often see riders collapse on landing and not give their horses clear direction as to what is next. I love using this exercise because I am able to give riders a clear plan, which teaches them to be a "thinking rider" throughout an entire series of jumps instead of through just one line.

Just as this exercise helps the rider become more organized, it does the same thing for the horse, as he is forced to regroup and reorganize during his circles between the cones. Whether you have an Advanced horse that likes to land off a jump and take over, or a "greenie" that tends to land in a heap, the middle circle helps the horse organize his body and tune back in to the rider, before carrying on to the next obstacle.

/ HOW

As part of your warm-up, introduce the first skill needed to make this exercise successful. Ask your horse to lengthen the canter, then quietly come to a halt from a simple voice command. Depending on whether you routinely use voice commands or not, it can take a few times for this new "button" to be installed.

Once your horse is halting fairly reliably based on the voice command, switch direction and again lengthen the canter, but this time collect the canter on a small circle then halt on the circle, still using the voice as the main aid to create the halt.

Once you are warmed up, start off by jumping the straight line of oxers (Jumps A and B). Count how many strides you got the first time through. Then, simply change direction and canter the straight line of oxers on the other lead, and once again count your strides. Often it will be different, which is to be expected as horses, just like people, often are dominant on one side. It is your job as a rider to try to get your horse to be as even and balanced on both sides as possible, which you will work on throughout this exercise.

The next step will seem overly simple but can be deceptively hard. Replicate the striding you just had between Jumps A and B. When the striding remains the same, great! This means you and your horse communicate well and are on the same page. When the striding is different, it means you need to work on being clear with your horse about what you're asking him. Thankfully, this exercise has a lot of opportunities to improve these lines of communication.

Before moving on to the next piece of the exercise, fit in an even number of strides based on your particular horse's stride length between Jump A and B. The first step to helping this happen is to make sure the distance is set up appropriately for the size of the arena, and that the cones are in place from the beginning. When the arena is smaller (closer to 120 feet in length), the distance should be closer to 80 feet. And when the arena is larger (more than 126 feet in length), the oxers should be set closer to the 86-foot distance. From here, you should find the most appropriate canter and number of strides for your level, which means you may

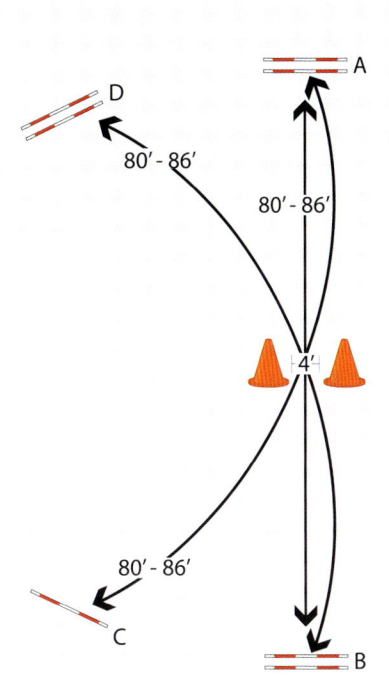

need to encourage your horse to open his step, or you may need to encourage him to shorten his step. Regardless of which situation you are in, the key will be keeping the canter consistent and rhythmic. And the key to a consistent horse is to be a consistent rider!

Once you are jumping from Jump A to B and vice versa on a straight line in a consistent number of strides, start to utilize the two cones in the middle of the oxers. To start, jump the first oxer (Jump A or B) then circle between the cones on whatever lead you land on. Ideally, the jumps will be set in the center of the ring, or minimally on the quarterline so you can approach and leave the exercise from either direction.

THE EXERCISES

Then start to get picky and dictate the direction of the circle as you approach the first jump. If you land on the wrong lead, come to a trot before the cones, and pick up the correct lead at the start of your circle. No matter what setup you have, remain on that circle until you can maintain an even canter, then continue on to the second oxer.

For younger or more inexperienced horses, it may take a few circles to get organized, but don't circle too much as young horses often have a hard time maintaining a balanced canter for long periods of time.

Regardless of the level or type of horse, I find this center circle is extremely helpful. For example, my World Equestrian Games partner Fernhill Fearless ("Sparky") can often land, then try to take over. The center circle forces him to pay attention and remain rideable. To keep things even more interesting for Sparky, and some of my other more advanced horses, I will land and circle on the counter-canter, and maybe throw in a flying change to the correct lead before continuing on to the next step.

When you are riding on your own, you need to think about what skills you need to work on as opposed to what you find easy. If your horse tends to get strong between fences, force yourself to throw in a canter-to-trot or canter-to-walk transition on the circle for a few steps before picking up the canter again and continuing on. On the flip side, if your horse is slow off your leg, ask him for a few steps of medium canter on the circle before continuing. Remember, you will only get better when you challenge yourself and your horse!

Once you have mastered the straight line of oxers (Jumps A and B) with the circle in the middle, start to incorporate the two jumps (Jumps C and D) on the sides. Make up a course of four to six jumps and incorporate two to three circles in the course. For example, you can start with Jump A, circle, and continue right to Jump C, turn left and jump Jump B with a bending line to Jump D, and finish by continuing to the right to jump Jump A, circle and finish over Jump B. The possibilities are really endless, so use your imagination to create your own course.

As you can imagine, this is a great exercise for riders who struggle to remember courses because you can really break things down into pieces, then build on each piece until you have a mini course. As mentioned earlier, I also find that this exercise really helps riders who struggle to keep riding beyond the first jump on course. The circles are perfect for helping these riders regroup and reorganize so they feel prepared for the next part of the course. This exercise is also really excellent for people who just need to slow their minds down. ◆

GRID PRO QUO / Margaret Rizzo McKelvy /

EXERCISE EXPERT

Cavalletti and Coursework

Brett Shear-Heyman

of Penny Leigh, LLC, in Middleburg, Virginia

For the rider, this exercise focuses on finding a good rhythm and concentrating on straightness. For the horse, this exercise teaches a bit of responsibility for his own body as well as correct jumping style.

/ MATERIALS NEEDED

- 4 cavalletti

OR

- 4 jump poles and 4 sets of standards

/ SETUP

- You can set this up anywhere in your arena, including either long side or across the diagonal.

▽ **About the expert:**

Brett Shear-Heyman is a hunter-jumper trainer and rider based in Middleburg, Virginia. She is passionate about developing horses and riders through simple exercises and positive experiences. With over 15 years of professional experience training all levels of hunters and jumpers, she aims to help her clients and horses find success and enjoyment out of learning. ◆

www.pennyleighllc.com

- While cavalletti are shown in the diagram, you can be flexible with what you use for the obstacles. Anything from ground poles to verticals are appropriate.

- If you have a short-strided horse or a pony, set the lines at 42 or 43 feet to make it more comfortable.

- For a horse with a big stride, set the lines to 45 feet, and feel free to open the bounce beyond 10 feet. You do not want your horse to feel claustrophobic.

/ WHY

I love this exercise because it can be adjusted for a lot of different goals. Ultimately, the two things you will always focus on to get a great jump out of your horse are *rhythm* and *track*. This grid asks you to address both. You can set this exercise with poles on the ground, small cavalletti, or larger verticals, depending on the level of you and your horse.

    I like this exercise because it asks the rider to answer certain questions, but it also encourages the horse to learn from the system and become a bit more independent. The exercise requires the rider to develop the correct canter to properly measure the line. The correct canter may vary depending on the number of steps you are aiming for, and you will learn to recognize the range in your canter. You are also responsible for straightness. While that principle may seem basic, it is essential.

    For the horse, it encourages correct jumping style and smoothness. It will be evident if your horse is rushing the grid. The middle element, the bounce, will help teach him to jump in correct style as he will be encouraged to slow down and take his time without you doing all the work. If you have a more sluggish horse, the bounce will encourage a bit of dexterity and activate his hind end to build strength. This is the part of the exercise where we hope to see the horse process the information and independently answer the questions correctly.

/ HOW

Warm up all the different gears you may need while on the flat. Once you consider your horse to be warm and prepared, begin the exercise.

GRID PRO QUO / *Margaret Rizzo McKelvy* /

For your first experience over this grid, set the entire exercise with poles on the ground. Usually, you can raise the height of the elements quite quickly, but always start with everything on the ground.

Begin by cantering the entire exercise. Because the measurement of the line is 45 feet, you can do either three or four strides. I suggest starting with four, which will require a compact, powerful canter. The canter should be established in the turn before you approach the first element. Your aim should be to meet the bounce portion softly without any change in rhythm. If you are still pulling on the reins to fit in the fourth stride, the bounce will inevitably ride long. If you prepare early, you can allow your horse to use a bit of scope to make the bounce comfortable.

Then, prepare for the four strides after the bounce. If your horse rushes the line, you need to compress his stride early. If your horse needs a bit of forward focus, add leg to comfortably canter the final element.

Once you're satisfied with the exercise as a four-stride exercise, try it with three strides instead. This is when I typically open up the bounce to 10 feet.

To accomplish this as a three-stride exercise, it is important to have the correct canter. Only lengthening after the first element is not how you leave a stride out. It is done by establishing the right stride length *before the turn to the first element*. If your canter is not correct, you will find yourself long and weak jumping into the bounce portion. But when you create a good canter early, the three strides will ride well.

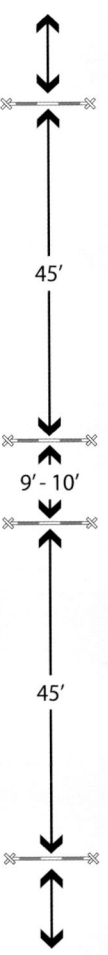

THE EXERCISES

Ideally, the bounce element will teach your horse one of two things, depending on his way of going: For a forward horse, it will encourage him to slow his jump and take his time at the base, even out of a big powerful canter. For a sluggish horse, it will encourage cleverness and strengthen his hind end. As a rider, your job is to let the bounce do the work. Try to stay out of your horse's way and focus on your position.

Once you land after the bounce, you'll have to reestablish the needed canter to properly meet the final element. Hold your position here, and if you need to lengthen the stride again, do it with your leg and a light seat as opposed to sitting heavily in the saddle.

In a perfect world, the horse holds one lead through the whole grid. If not, do not worry or drill your horse, just appreciate that your horse is trying to find his balance. Consider how you might be able to help him with your body by staying more centered or being conscious of his straightness.

If you're looking for a challenge, switch between doing four and three strides. Also, you can play with using poles as the first and last element, and cavalletti or jumps as the middle elements. Everything can be tailored to the specific training goals for each horse and rider.

Ultimately, you'll learn so much about your rhythm and track by riding this grid. Even tiny-tot kiddos can trot over this grid as poles to practice holding their position and keeping their ponies straight. ◆

EXERCISE

Cavalletti and Turning

EXPERT

Eric Smiley

of Little Beerland in Bridport, Dorset, England

These exercises help riders stop obsessing about getting the "perfect spot," and instead focus on finding the perfect canter. The repetitive nature of the exercises will help riders find just the right canter.

/ MATERIALS NEEDED

- 7 ground poles or cavalletti
- 4 jump poles
- 4 sets of standards

/ SETUP

- It is important to measure the distances exactly for this exercise. Everything is based on a 20-meter circle, which is converted to feet in the diagram.

- Your oxers (Exercise 2) can be placed in the same arena, as long as they are out of the way of your cavalletti.

▽ **About the expert:**

Eric Smiley is a former international event rider who represented Ireland at European, World, and Olympic level, winning team bronze medals on two occasions. Eric began his equestrian career in the Pony Club and continued it in the army and then the world-renowned Talland Equestrian Center, during which time he gained his British Horse Society Instructor's certificate. In 1995, he passed his British Horse Society Fellowship exam, the highest teaching qualification in the industry. He was Team Coach to the Belgian eventing team for the 2011 European Eventing Championships and 2012 London Olympics and is an FEI judge who regularly acts as a Ground Jury member. Eric is the author of the cross-country bible *Look… No Hands!*; *Two Brains, One Aim*; and *The Sport Horse Problem Solver*. He travels the globe helping professional and amateur riders achieve their goals. ◆

www.ericsmiley.co.uk

/ WHY

With all riders, the source of greatest concern is the "arrival in front of the jump." Much is taught about how to get there, and more often than not, this adds to the confusion. The mere mentioning of the subject can bring a glazed look to most riders.

These exercises allow riders to manage their canter, and to become more confident in its repetition and the knowledge that their horse can jump from this canter. The focus then changes to the canter between jumps and not the arrival. The arrival will look after itself.

/ HOW

Before you even start the first exercise, you need to take a moment to understand the geometry. The two 20-meter circles are touching, which means that the radius from the center is 10 meters. The poles are placed at each circle point, with the diameter from the center of the poles on either side being 20 meters. The circumference of the circle is 63 meters, with there being 15.75 meters between each pole. While all of these numbers may seem a little intimidating on paper, this is a shape that is familiar to most riders.

Note: *The distances have been converted to feet in the diagram for Exercise 1.*

This is a fundamental shape and size you can find in any discipline, whether it be a dressage test, show jumping course, or out on cross-country. It is important to know the measurements so that you can begin to relate distances to the feel of your horse's canter. And by doing this, you can better understand the relationship between the canter and the jump.

Begin by cantering a circle with two ground poles, then three poles, and then all four poles. With all the poles on the ground, fit four strides between each one. Your goal is to be able to canter with regularity and fit four strides between the poles over and over until it becomes easy. This is an exercise where you will find success by being proactive in riding the canter, versus letting the exercise happen to you.

The next step with this exercise is to ride the outside line—simply the circle created by the outer edges of the ground poles—fitting five even and

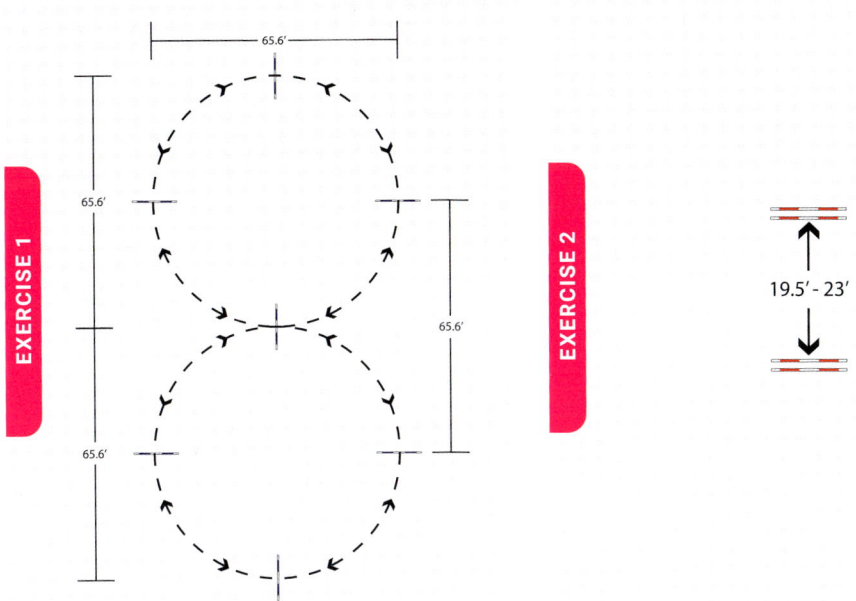

regular strides between each pole. Then, while still staying on this outside line, open up your canter to fit four strides in. And then shorten your canter and move back to your centerline, cantering over the poles with four strides between them.

By playing around with the different canter between the different lines, work on developing a feel for the appropriate canter in relation to your distances.

If you are a more advanced rider and want to challenge yourself, make these ground poles into small 18-inch jumps. Just be careful to not raise them all at once, and instead do so gradually.

By raising the ground poles to small jumps, your horse will get used to jumping from a managed canter and you get used to being patient. Be sure to remain in a light seat once the ground poles are raised into small jumps. A light seat allows your horse the freedom to jump and encourages you to find your balance.

If you're at a level where flying changes are part of your routine, make the center pole where the circles touch into a small jump appropriate for your level. This will allow you to practice your lead changes over the jump.

After you've successfully completed the circle exercise, you're ready for your line of oxers, as illustrated by Exercise 2. While these two oxers may seem simple on paper, they are full of variables. Depending on your horse and what you're trying to accomplish that day, you can

THE EXERCISES

adjust the distance between the jumps, adjust the width of the oxers, or adjust the height of the oxers.

If you want to encourage your horse to be a little tidier and work on compressing his stride, leave the distance between the two closer to 6 meters or 19 feet 6 inches. But if you have a horse that tends to back off and not use himself to the full scope of his step, leave the distance closer to 7 meters or 23 feet.

This is when having educated eyes on the ground can help you in adjusting the fences to suit you and your horse on that given day. The goal is to encourage carefulness and scope, to encourage the horse to react to what he sees, and to help him become more physically and mentally athletic.

If for whatever reason you need to increase the intensity of these oxers, you can add placing poles before and after the jump. But be careful not to confuse or over-face your horse by doing so. You always want to encourage confidence so placing poles must be used with care. ◆

EXERCISE

Coursework and Turning

EXPERT

Allison Springer

of Allison Springer Eventing in Upperville, Virginia

This exercise helps riders work on being able to create and maintain the proper canter needed for a variety of questions, which helps the horse work on his shape and technique over fences.

/ MATERIALS NEEDED

- 11 jump poles
- 1 skinny jump pole
- 1 heavy gate
- 12 sets of standards
- 1 corner stand

/ SETUP

- To set this course up completely you need an arena that is minimally 112 feet in length.

- If you are working with a smaller area, you can adjust the distances or only set up portions of what is depicted here.

▽ **About the expert:**

A consummate athlete and compassionate rider, Allison is a popular clinician, traveling throughout the country to teach each year. Her classic position and strong fundamentals highlight her talent, poise, and partnership with the horse. Known for her dedication, Allison has been consistently named to the United States Equestrian Federation's High Performance Training Lists, a proven training ground for national team riders, and she was also shortlisted for the London Olympic Games. ◆

www.allisonspringer.com

THE EXERCISES

- If you don't have corner stands, you can use an extra standard, barrel, or upside-down muck tub.

/ WHY

I use this course, and especially this grid, often because of its versatility and the countless options available for riders of all skill levels. Overall, this setup is meant to help horses with their technique and riders with both their position and ability to create and maintain the correct canter for the questions they are asking of their horse.

The distances in the grid encourage the horse to get a bit deeper to the final jump in the line, which challenges the rider to be confirmed in her equitation and her ability to keep the horse in balance for the final jump. The grid really teaches the rider and horse to not only become comfortable with the final stride being slightly shorter than the stride before but also how to get a great jump from that moment.

One of two things often go through a rider's head a couple of strides away from the jump: "Thank goodness," or, "Oh, geez." It's when those "Oh, geez" moments occur, which typically arise from not knowing when the horse is going to leave the ground, that riders need to be in the best mindset for their horses. The rider needs to stay confirmed in her position and maintain the horse's balance and also keep her leg on so the horse has the ability to negotiate a long or short distance well.

Too often in these "Oh, geez" moments we see riders "go fetal" (dropping their hands, leaning forward, and taking their legs off), which in turn encourages a bad jump: a chip, a stop, or a discombobulated attempt from a long distance.

Remember the horse always mirrors the rider's body position so if you "go fetal" in one of those "Oh, geez" moments, you are asking your horse to suddenly change his balance by getting on his forehand, sticking his hind end out behind him, all the while allowing him to get behind your leg because you took it away. This isn't the best recipe for success!

/ HOW

When warming up, take a minute or two to focus on your leg position. The foot should be at about a 45-degree angle away from the horse's side with a little bit of weight on the inside of the stirrup. When looking at your leg, you should be able to see a slice of the sole of your boot from the side, which creates a secure calf-to-ankle connection with the horse's side.

Test yourself by maintaining this leg position in two-point position, at the halt and then back to full seat. Too often you see people get in two-point position by taking their leg totally off the horse, standing up, and losing the connection. With enough attention to your leg position on the flat, it will start to become a habit, which will only help you over fences.

Then, review how your full seat is different in a jumping saddle as compared to a dressage saddle, with your upper body being slightly more forward in a jumping saddle. This is very important because when you get behind the motion on the flat before a jump, it's much more challenging to be with the motion over the jump.

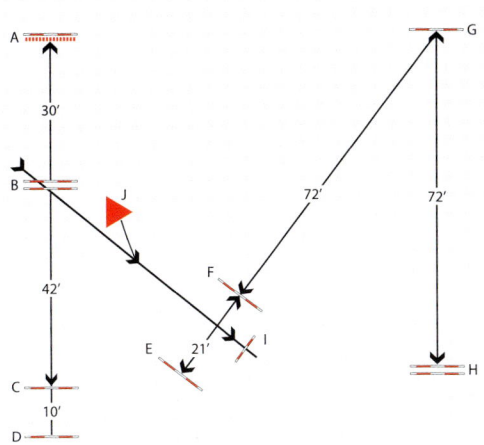

I encourage my students to practice and make the automatic release a habit, which I believe to be safest for event riders, especially while riding on varying terrain. I always encourage an athletic stance and tell my students that if they were ever to be dropped out of the sky, they should easily land in an athletic stance over their feet.

And to round out your rider-position checklist, look to your arms. Your lower arm needs to always be in line with where you want the horse's mouth to be, with your elbow slightly in front of their shoulder. This position allows for a much more elastic arm. With this arm position and the correct rein length, you should easily be able to grab mane when in a jumping position, and if you can't, then your reins are probably too long or you are not in a good athletic stance.

In terms of what you're looking for from your horse, work on your horse's adjustability by making sure he can lengthen and shorten his stride easily and rhythmically within each gait. Remember that the dial for collection is different than the dial for speed. Maintaining the tempo along with varying lengths of stride is a crucial skill in creating the correct canter for the jump. Once you can create the correct canter and maintain the rules of the canter to the jump while maintaining a good position, your horse should be able to negotiate a range of distances well. Do this consistently and you will learn to develop a correct eye for a distance.

Initially, don't try to have an eye to a fence, because everyone has a "fabulous" eye one-to-two strides away, but then it's too late to make a change, though it's not too late to be aware of the situation you're in. Instead, focus on having and maintaining a good canter. As the rider, it's your job to create the length of stride that's appropriate for the job at hand. You will need a different canter for a 10-foot bounce (Jumps C and D) than you will for a 30-foot combination (Jumps A and B), and a different canter for a 21-foot one-stride (Jumps E and F) than a skinny or corner (Jumps I or J) off a long approach. Learning which canter you need for each situation, then being able to seamlessly change from one canter to the next, are keys to jumping success.

After you've effectively and efficiently warmed up at the canter, you're ready to start jumping! Start by using the bounce (Jumps C and D) of the grid line (I typically have them set as cross-rails), then simply canter over them on a circle— first to the left away from the rest of the grid, then to the right.

THE EXERCISES

175 /

I like to warm up over the bounce because bounces are good for rider position. If you fold too early or too much, you end up with your horse's head in your face. To avoid this, concentrate on letting your arm follow the horse's mouth, not on how much you fold. You want to be able to land balanced over your leg with your horse in the same canter as the approach.

After you've done this in both directions, jump through the whole grid (from Jump D to C to B to A) at a low warm-up height. It's not uncommon for the horse not to be prepared to go straight after the bounce since he has been circling over it a few times, so be prepared to steer.

Once he gets the idea that he is now going straight, you'll start to feel the importance of landing in balance and stretching your upper body tall. I like to tell my students to land as if they're riding straight out of the ring, with eyes up and shoulders tall.

I gradually raise the oxer (Jump B) a little and the final heavy gate (Jump A) a bit more to where the horse and rider are really challenged to land in balance from the oxer and keep the horse connected and straight for the final heavy gate.

The distance between Jump B and A is only 30 feet, which feels very short after riding the bounce and the flowing three strides to Jump B. The straightness over Jump A is incredibly important because you do not want to allow your horse to deal with a tighter distance by drifting or getting crooked. If he is consistently kept straight, he will jump higher and learn excellent technique.

Once you've jumped through this gymnastic line a few times, start to make small courses with the other jumps.

The 72-foot line between Jump G and H is always a super easy and wonderful number to practice if you have the space in your arena. It can be five or six strides and is a good way to improve adjustability between jumps.

Your 21-foot one-stride between Jump E and F is a great place to practice riding to a deep distance.

And the angled line from Jump B to Jump I is where speed and line of direction come in. Sometimes, jumping angled fences can give the rider some anxiety, but if you can remember to keep the rules the same, you will have success.

Overall, jumping questions are made easier by the rider's understanding of how to make the right canter for the horse and for that particular question, and by maintaining her correct position. Riders need to be able to give their horses all the ingredients they need to succeed. Often, this can be done by going back to the basics. ◆

EXERCISE EXPERT

Coursework and Traditional Gymnastic

Sheryl Sutherby

of Rolling Acres Show Stables in Brookeville, Maryland

/ MATERIALS NEEDED

- 2 ground poles
- 2 cavalletti
- 4 jump poles
- 4 sets of standards

/ SETUP

- These exercises can be set up all at once next to each other, or you can adjust one exercise to become the next as you go.

- To keep things simple between Exercise 1 and 2, you can use cavalletti on their lowest setting for Exercise 1 instead of separate ground poles.

- To keep things simple between Exercise 3 and 4, you can simply have a ground person move the jumps.

▽ **About the expert:**

A lifelong horsewoman, Sheryl Sutherby has been a part of the Rolling Acres Show Stables team since 2001. In addition to managing the barn, she is an active member of the training and instruction team at this top A-circuit barn. After earning her BS in Computer Science from the University of Maryland, she worked in corporate America for several years before deciding to leave to follow her passion with horses. Sheryl is an 'R' hunter and equitation judge and a USHJA Certified Trainer. ◆

www.rollingacresshowstables.com

THE EXERCISES

/ WHY

This is a classic exercise that I like to incorporate into my lessons throughout the year. While some may find it easy to change the number of strides between jumps, the key here is for the rider to learn to differentiate between the pace needed for five strides versus the pace needed for seven strides.

The ability to adjust your horse's stride throughout a course is imperative to finding success in the show ring. You'll find this impossible if you don't think about your striding until you're in the air over your first jump. You need to make your changes before you even enter the corner before the jump. The key to success here is to make a plan, then prepare far enough in advance to execute that plan.

/ HOW

After you've warmed up lightly, go ahead and canter over your poles on the ground as illustrated in Exercise 1. Your first goal is to get five even strides, center to center, between your ground poles. With these just being poles on the ground, resist the urge to get too busy in the saddle. Instead, focus on being still in the saddle and feeling your horse underneath you.

As you go through the ground poles, give yourself time to reflect on any mistakes before

EXERCISE 1

60'

EXERCISE 2

60'

GRID PRO QUO / *Margaret Rizzo McKelvy* /

coming to them again. If your horse took off too early, try sitting up a bit taller the next time. If your horse chipped in, try adding a little more leg. If your horse met the second pole on a half-stride, try closing your leg on landing and riding him into a contact. Mistakes are fine, it's what you learn from them that matters.

Once you are consistently and confidently fitting five strides between the jumps, choose between starting to play with your striding, or moving on to your cavalletti (Exercise 2), then your small verticals (2 foot 6 inches or below; Exercise 3), and finally your larger verticals (2 feet 9 inches or above; Exercise 4).

Assuming you're going to start playing around with your striding, you can stick with Exercise 1 for a little longer and try to fit in six strides between your poles, then alternate between five and six strides. More advanced pairs can aim to add a seven-stride option into the mix.

Remember you need to adjust your canter before you even get to the corner before the jumps. You need to constantly be thinking ahead, which can be a challenge. Don't forget to breathe as you work your way through these exercises.

Once you're able to consistently and confidently change your striding in harmony with your horse through Exercise 1, you're ready to challenge yourself by moving on to playing with striding over the cavalletti (Exercise 2), then the two small verticals (Exercise 3), and finally the two larger verticals (Exercise 4). As you move

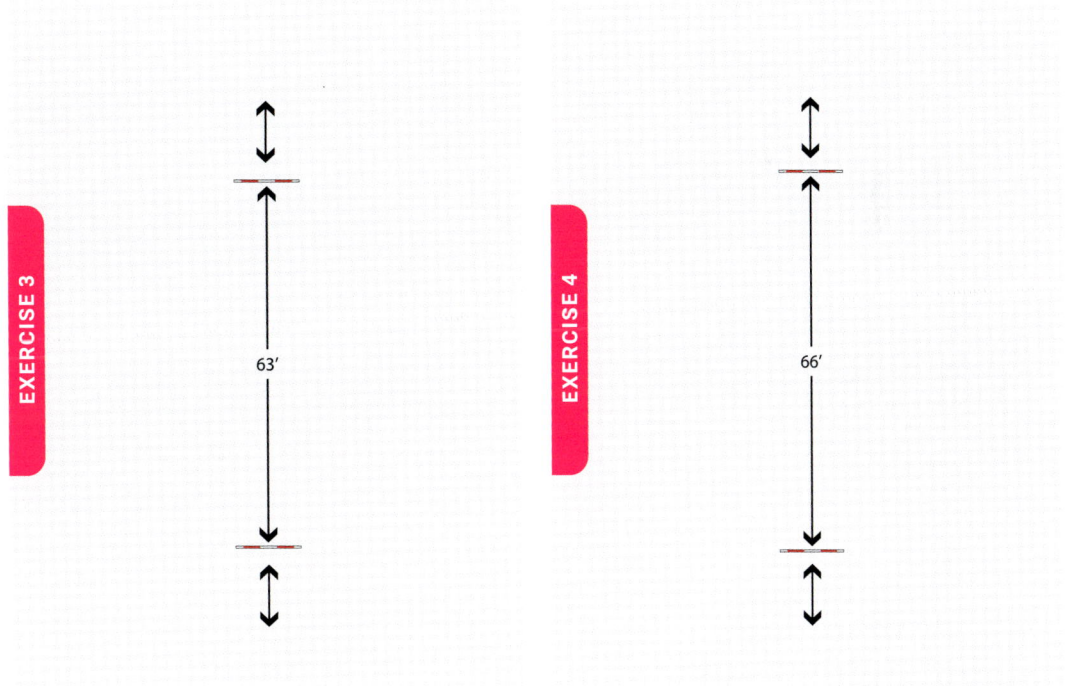

THE EXERCISES

your way through the exercises, change directions often so that you're working both sides of your horse.

At all times, make sure your horse is understanding the changes you're asking for and isn't resentful. If your horse gets a little grouchy or undone at any time, change the subject by doing something easier, and gradually go back to what you were trying to accomplish.

As you alternate your striding, keep in mind that fitting seven even, rhythmic strides requires a lot of collection, which requires a lot of leg but also means you need to close your fingers around the reins to encourage your horse to close his step a little.

Whenever you ask your horse to open up for the five strides, concentrate on not allowing him to get flat. To do this, make sure his energy is coming from your leg and he is lengthening his strides from behind, and not simply stiffening his frame while getting flat.

Regardless of your level, set realistic goals for yourself. If you're a more novice rider, concentrate on your five-stride option, then your six-stride option. But if you're a more advanced rider, challenge yourself by alternating your striding each time through. ◆

EXERCISE

Cavalletti and Turning

EXPERT

Meghan Truppner

of Karmic Run Stables in Mount Airy, Maryland

This combination of cavalletti and ground poles helps the rider work on creating a better balance in her horse through a series of straight lines, turns, and transitions. The focus on transitions really puts a lot of pressure on the rider to work on her accuracy and her horse's responsiveness.

/ MATERIALS NEEDED

- 9 ground poles or cavalletti

/ SETUP

- You have the choice of using ground poles or cavalletti here.
- This exercise is best set up in the center of your arena but can easily fit on one short side as long as you leave the rail clear.

▽ **About the expert:**

A lifelong horsewoman, Meghan Truppner is based out of her own Karmic Run Stables in Mount Airy, Maryland. She truly believes that any horse and any rider can do dressage and you can find horses and riders of all different skill levels at her farm. Professionally, Meghan has competed through the FEI levels of dressage on a variety of horses, and has spent time studying rider biomechanics, in-hand training, and natural horsemanship. Meghan prides herself in the ability to teach the biomechanics and "whys" of dressage to riders in a way that not only makes sense to them, but also makes sense to their horses. Spend a day with Meghan and you'll learn that every rider who comes to her is given a fair shot at achieving her dreams. ◆

www.karmicrun.com

/ WHY

This exercise—known as "The Spider" in my barn—is one of my absolute favorites. It is easy to set up and doesn't require a lot of equipment, plus it can be introduced on the longe line, if needed. This setup is designed to facilitate better balance while combining straight lines, turns, up-and-down transitions, along with counting steps. You can ride quite a few different combinations within a short period of time, thus maximizing the value of each step.

Chances are you've heard of the importance of transitions at some point during your riding career. And while I agree that transitions are important, I believe that the word "transition" can be lost in translation, thus losing its significance when not thought of properly. If I ask you for a trot-canter-trot transition without further instruction, most riders would put harmony at the top of their priority list. And while I agree that harmony should be a top priority, if that is the only priority, the transition itself can often fade a bit, with a loss of balance, often causing the rider to take on more responsibility for the horse's body. And thus a cycle begins.

However, if I ask you to make five steps of trot, to seven strides of canter, and then five steps of trot, and so on, the intention changes. Now, while still striving for harmony, it is no

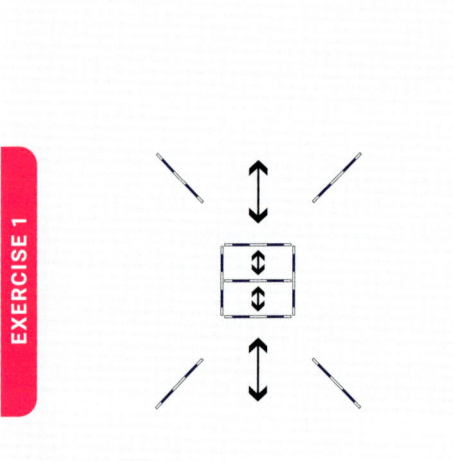

EXERCISE 1

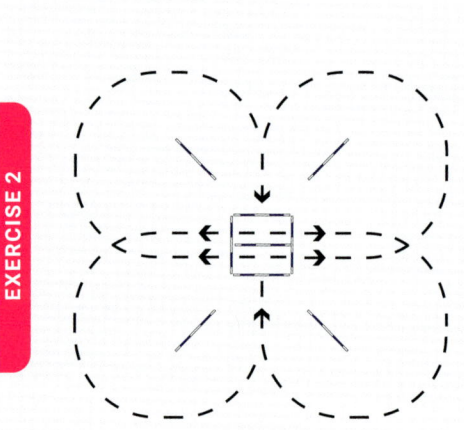

EXERCISE 2

longer the number one priority. Now the top priority is adjustability, and a horse that can easily change his sacroiliac joint to switch his steps from trot to canter and back again. As a rider, the key is that these transitions are being made in balance with your seat, which will go a long way to achieve harmony.

While dressage is my first love, I teach a variety of students with several competing at the upper levels of their sports, and I can tell you that all my students agree that this exercise helps with their jumping. Regardless of the sport that we choose to compete in, we're all in a never-ending quest for balance, seamless transitions, and harmony. The more harmonious we are with our horses, the happier they are, and the happier our horses are, the harder they will want to work for us.

/ HOW

Always start with something your horse has seen before and build from there. In this case start with Exercise 1. The three trot poles on the centerline offer your horse a nice, easy, rhythmic start. I did not include measurements here on purpose as I want you to set them to suit your horse. Typically, trot poles are placed in the 4- to 5-foot range. Don't be afraid to adjust as you go!

Once your horse is accustomed to this, add in Exercise 2, which adds in left and right turns after the trot poles in a clover leaf pattern around

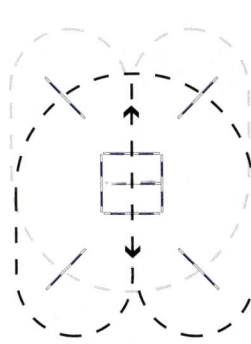

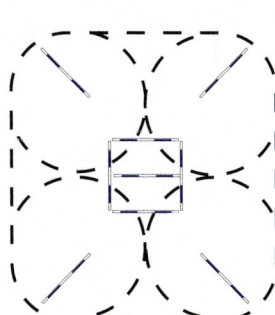

the "legs" of the spider, leading you back through the box laterally. Try to alternate which lane you go to and make a mental note of any differences you feel. If your horse isn't quite on your aids yet, throw in a halt transition in your box, and then transition back up on your way out of the box. These halt transitions help activate your horse's hind leg, as halting in a confined space is challenging and requires your horse to lift his shoulders to successfully transition out of the box.

Your next step is Exercise 3 and the overall shape of this pattern is a heart shape or cardioid. You begin by trotting your three poles, then transitioning to your canter as soon as you leave the box and circle over two of your "spider legs," before transitioning back to the trot to go through your three poles again. To challenge yourself, try and play around with where you make your transitions, but be very precise about where you want to make the transition and stick to it. In general, the closer you are to a ground pole in a transition, the more your horse will have to balance on his hindquarters and be quicker in his response to your aids.

And don't forget to have fun with this exercise! Horses are puzzles, and it's your job as the rider to figure out how to put them together.

If your transitions have been honest, this should be easy. If your transitions haven't been honest, you're about to find out, at which point you can go back a step and repeat it until it's easy.

Move on to Exercise 4, which is trotting, then cantering, through the corners of the box and around each "spider leg." Be sure to give your horse the appropriate space needed for each gait, so you'll stay closer to the point of the corner in the trot, but closer to the center of the box in the canter.

Now you can put it all together and change directions through the trot poles or the lanes, perhaps even throwing in a flying-lead change if it's in your toolbox. The goal is to put all the pieces together into a course, complete with specific points for your transitions.

And while this exercise can be ridden without stopping, you can also ride in and out of each element if you want to—or need to—work on something else. ◆

EXERCISE EXPERT

Coursework and Turning

Skyeler Voss

of Morningside Eventing in The Plains, Virginia

Regardless of your discipline, having good instincts with a quick reaction time are vital to your success in any jumping arena. This exercise puts together a few patterns to educate riders and help them work on the skills needed for their horses to carefully execute a series of bending lines and turns.

/ MATERIALS NEEDED

- 1 ground pole
- 8 jump poles
- 7 sets of standards

/ SETUP

- The distances here are merely suggestions. Everything can be easily adjusted to fit into your space. The exercise is best completed with a ground person.

▽ **About the expert:**

Skyeler Voss, an Advanced-level rider, is the founder and head trainer at Morningside Eventing in The Plains, Virginia. For over 20 years she has trained and competed numerous horses through the international levels. While riding and training horses is a priority for Skyeler, teaching has always been her passion, and she enjoys instructing riders of every level and age. ◆

www.morningsideeventingteam.com

- Once you have everything set, place all your jump poles on the ground except for Jump A with the preceding ground pole.

/ WHY

Event riders pride themselves on the quick instincts and reaction time that are imperative when tackling the toughest of cross-country combinations or the most technical of show jump courses. And while I use this exercise in my eventing program, I believe that riders of all disciplines can benefit from it.

Riders build their skills from hours in the saddle and practicing technical questions in controlled environments. Most grids are in straight lines and help to change a horse's shape, a rider's position, or a variation in stride lengths. This exercise is quite different, focusing on the rider's reactions, concentration, and correct execution of bending lines and turns. It helps a rider understand both sides of the horse when tighter turns are involved, and it requires accuracy on the takeoff, in the air, and on landing. It highlights the necessary ambidexterity of both horse and rider in the modern-day sport of eventing and technical cross-country courses.

I've provided recommended distances here, but this is one of those exercises that can be adjusted to fit your space and your horse's level of training. Don't be scared to change things up a bit.

/ HOW

To start off, always warm up on the flat, being careful to incorporate the necessary turning skills needed for this exercise. Focus on circles and turns to hone in on the importance of the outside aids and the correct position of bend. The focus is on bending the horse through the rib cage and not just the neck—this helps make sure that your whole horse is between your aids. Also work on establishing a correct half-halt so that you are competent enough to keep your horse coming forward from behind when the tight turns are added.

Once you are warmed up with your horse properly on the aids, trot and then canter a simple cross-rail (Jump A) with a placement rail 8 to 9 feet in front. You'll keep jumping the cross-rail until you can land in a straight line and keep a consistent rhythm before and after the jump. The placement rail before the jump will help set you up for success.

After you've jumped Jump A from either direction a few times, start working on Jump B and C on the bending line. To begin, you'll want to leave the rails on the ground. Make sure that you can jump the cross-rail and land with your horse straight between your aids. Then you can start to ask your horse to land and canter two bending strides to the left for Jump C, then two bending strides to the right for Jump B.

Most horses have a dominant direction, so be sure to school these turns and help them feel the correct line on both sides. Additionally, most riders have a dominant direction, so by switching directions each time, you will help yourself become more comfortable and competent in both directions.

After you're easily jumping this first bending line (Jump A to Jump B or C), raise the ground rails at Jump B or C to two slanted verticals, with the inside portion lower than the outside portion. The reason for the slant is to encourage the rider to turn sharply rather than just letting the horse drift through the outside aids. If the horse escapes out the outside shoulder, the rider will find herself at the higher end of the jump.

The height of the vertical at Jumps B and C is in direct correlation with the horse-and-rider's competence level. Typically, make the tall side no bigger than the maximum height that the rider is comfortable jumping.

Once you begin to understand the turns and are able to execute the proper bending line, you can begin to play with the fun part of the question.

At this point, you'll need your instructor or ground person to stand directly between Jump

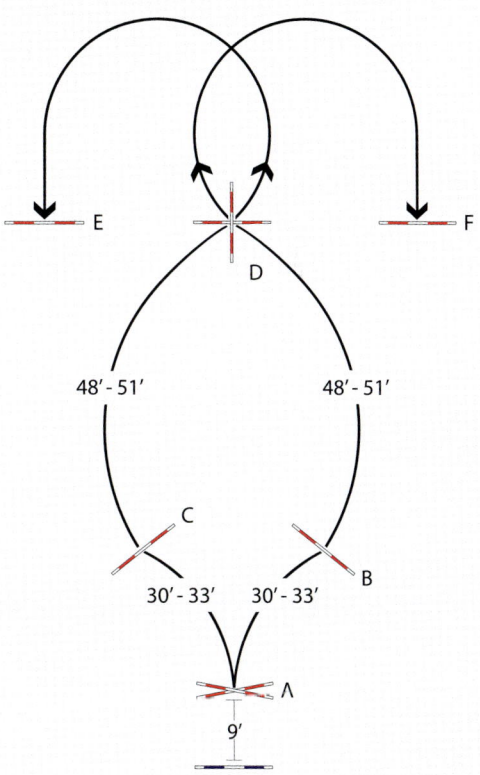

THE EXERCISES

B and C. As you approach the placing rail in front of Jump A, your instructor will point right or left. You then have to be able to react quickly and make the correct turn. As you get better with your reaction time, start to challenge yourself by having your instructor wait until you are in the air over Jump A to receive your direction. It is important that the jump size is well within the horse and rider's repertoire, as mistakes are inevitable and you don't want to get into too much trouble while you're learning.

Now you can add in the cat's cradle (Jump D). This is simply a skinny jump in a different form. This jump highlights the importance of being able to keep your horse straight all the way through the bascule of the fence to the landing. While it looks intimidating, it jumps very nicely with your horse jumping across the center "X." If you're worried about it, start with a simple two rails on the ground and introduce this jump on its own by trotting then cantering it from all directions.

Finally, put the entire exercise together by having a ground person point left or right after Jump A to either Jump B or C. Jump the corresponding fence (Jump B if going right, and Jump C if going left) in the bending two strides, and then ride a four-to-five-stride bending line back to the cat's cradle (Jump D).

For an added challenge, place two verticals (Jump E and F) next to the cat's cradle. After you land from the cat's cradle, roll back to either Jump E or F set parallel to the cat's cradle. This turns it into more of a course-type question, which is great for riders getting ready to show.

When it is all put together, the rider should be able to have quick reflexes in both directions at the drop of a hat and be able to navigate a corresponding bending line to a narrow technical question. ◆

EXERCISE EXPERT

Coursework and Traditional Gymnastic

Danny Warrington

of LandSafe Equestrian in North East, Maryland

This is a great exercise to help teach the rider how to create a half-halt in between fences. It is also good for working on rider position, as well as the horse's canter.

/ MATERIALS NEEDED

- 5 to 10 jump poles
- 5 sets of standards
- 2 cones (optional)

/ SETUP

- The distances required here are typically too long to fit into an arena, so this is often best set up in a field.

- After you have everything set up, create a cross-rail for Jump A and put all the other jump poles to the side.

▽ **About the expert:**

Danny Warrington is a former leading steeplechase jockey turned international Advanced eventer. He has a deep passion for safety and personal responsibility that has led him to the creation of Land Safe Equestrian. Danny's goal is to bring riders as much knowledge in self-preservation as possible In a safe and controlled environment. He has spent years watching, studying, and developing an understanding of riders' reactions, both instinctual and learned. This gives him the ability to teach what is missing between reaction and response. ◆

www.landsafeequestrian.com

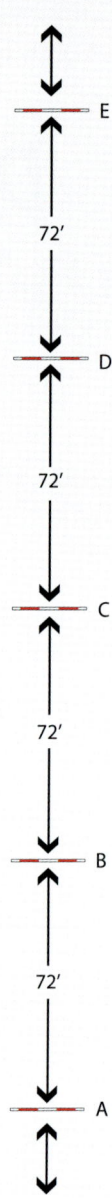

/ WHY

While I love traditional trot grids, I like this "fives" exercise because of everything it does for the rider. First off, unlike traditional trot grids where the jumps slow the horse down, this grid teaches the rider how to create the half-halt herself. And as others have mentioned, it is good to practice canter grids since all your coursework in competition is at the canter.

Finally, I've found this exercise to really help boost the rider's confidence. When you look down this long line of fences, it can look quite imposing, but after you break the exercise down and take it one jump at a time, it is quite doable. And when you have successfully completed the exercise, you look back and feel good about what you have accomplished.

/ HOW

Start with a simple cross-rail as Jump A. The height can vary depending on your comfort level, but I wouldn't make it any bigger than 2 feet 6 inches to start.

You'll want to trot in and halt before you reach the midway point to Jump B, which you can mark off with a line in the sand or a cone set off to the side. This may seem impossible at first but realize that you have a full two canter strides to create this halt, so while you can't take your time necessarily, you can land quietly then sit down in the saddle and ask for the halt.

If your horse blows through your halt transition, simply rein back until you're where you want to be. Repeat this exercise until you are

GRID PRO QUO / *Margaret Rizzo McKelvy* /

easily halting before the midway point; for some horses this will only take one or two repetitions, for others, you have to repeat this six or more times. Only once you can reliably halt after Jump A should you add in Jump B.

What you set up for Jump B and beyond is really up to you. If you're a more novice rider, you can set up another cross-rail as Jump B. If you're a more experienced rider, you can change Jump A to a vertical, then continue on with verticals down the rest of the line. The point is that this exercise isn't about the fences themselves but what happens *in between* them. So if you're most comfortable with cross-rails, set up all cross-rails. If you're most comfortable over 3-foot-6-inch verticals, then set that up.

As you're going through the beginning portions of this exercise, you want to feel your horse prepare for the halt on his own. So after you set up Jump B, come through another time or two where you land and halt after Jump A. Often a horse will see a jump in front of him and make a move toward it, so you want to make sure that your horse waits for you after each fence. This might mean that you have to wait a moment or two in the halt until your horse is standing stock still and takes a breath.

Once your horse prepares himself to halt after Jump A, you can land, half-halt, and continue on to Jump B. If your horse lands and doesn't respond to your half-halt, simply halt and repeat the exercise until he's listening again. Remember that at first you're trotting into the exercise, regardless of the fence height.

Once you're quietly jumping the first two fences, you can start cantering into the exercise. The same rules apply though. If your horse lands and runs through your half-halt, simply ask for a full halt. And if your horse doesn't halt until you're past the midway point between whatever jumps you're at, then rein back to that point.

It's important to never get impatient through this exercise. Most good horses want to go to their next fence with or without you, so it can be confusing at first for them to be asked to halt before their next fence. Just keep it simple and explain the exercise to your horse. Even if you need to break it down and simply canter over a pole on the ground and then halt, go ahead and do that. I would rather riders take that time than to be fighting with their horses through the exercise.

Once you're cantering through the first two fences, go ahead and add in Jumps C, D and E, one at a time. The hope is that your new and improved half-halt will continue to work after each fence. But if it does not work, go back to using the full halt, then trot or canter off to your next jump.

By the end of this exercise, you will find yourself riding very quietly, but still very forward to the fences. And your horse will learn to not rush between fences but instead to wait for your cue.

The first time you do this exercise, the simple five strides between each set of fences will be all you do. If you want a bigger challenge for the future, play with the striding between the fences. I typically don't try to put more than six strides between each jump, but for added complexity, put five strides between the first two jumps, six strides between the next set, then back to five strides.

The best part of this exercise is that you now have a new tool for use in competition: You will realize that you aren't helpless while on course and instead you *can* do something between fences. ◆

EXERCISE

Traditional Gymnastic

EXPERT

Whitney Weston

of Valkyrie Sporthorses in Southern Pines, North Carolina

This exercise is great if you're looking to set up one exercise that will meet the needs of a wide range of horses and riders. The focus is promoting relaxation between horse and rider.

▽ About the expert:

/ MATERIALS NEEDED

- 2 ground poles
- 3 jump poles
- 3 sets of standards
- 4 cones (optional)

/ SETUP

- This exercise does not take up a lot of room, so it will likely fit in most any arena.

- You have the option of putting pairs of cones at the beginning and end of your exercise to help with straightness.

A lifelong eventer, Whitney Weston is based in Southern Pines, North Carolina. With a career that has taken her all over the world, she boasts work experience with some of the world's best, including Phillip Dutton, Bruce Davidson, Buck Davidson, and Carol Gee, among others. Whitney has been able to build a loyal and loving base of students, clients, and owners while still maintaining a rigorous training and competition schedule. With her positive approach, Whitney gives riders of all levels a fun learning experience. ◆

www.valkyriesporthorses.com

/ WHY

There are several reasons why I love this exercise and why you will often find it set up in my jumping field. My barn has a wide variety of horses and riders, ranging from my Advanced competition horses to our youngest lesson students learning to trot their first cross-rails. This exercise has just enough variation to fit the needs of all our horses and riders. This comes in handy, as it would be exhausting to be setting up different exercises for all the horses throughout the day! The other great thing is that it doesn't take up a lot of room, so you can leave it set up for a while and set up a course around it.

This gymnastic aims to relax the horse and rider so the rider can focus on her position and following the horse, and the horse can relax and think more about his legs and form over fences. With simple distances and the little tweaks I will show you, it is a great exercise to create a connected yet relaxed canter. We often leave it set up in our arena so riders can establish their pace and connection, jump a course, then finish with this gymnastic again. The goal is to have the same canter throughout.

If your horse gets tense jumping a course, you can bring him back to this exercise at the end of the course to help him understand that all jumping is the same, whether a course or a predictable gymnastic.

/ HOW

Always try to keep things simple in the warm-up and focus on being able to hold your horse straight between your aids at all three gaits, with minimal hand involvement. Also, practice being able to easily switch from a posting trot to a two-point position, and at the canter being able to go from three different hip-angle positions: sitting, two-point, and a gallop position (a closed hip angle like a jockey). Not only does this help you stay loose in your joints, but it helps you realize how much your position can change your horse's rhythm. The end goal is to be able to switch from all these different positions without making a change to your horse's balance or rhythm.

Remember, it is your job to take care of prep work when it comes to jumping. Prep work involves having enough energy in the canter, making a nice balanced turn to the jump, keeping the horse straight, and supporting him with your leg. However, once you have successfully presented your horse to a jump, you need to move into a supportive role while your horse negotiates the obstacle. I find this way of thinking really benefits both horse and rider. The rider is able to concentrate on staying relaxed and balanced over her horse, and the horse is able to negotiate the jumping exercise with little interference from his rider. Of course, this is easier said than done!

Once you are properly warmed up, start Jump B as a ground pole and leave out Jump D entirely. This gives you three ground poles in a row. A series of poles at a somewhat varied distance can be enough to get your horse to think a little.

While warming up, put special emphasis on the turns before and after the exercise. Just like people, horses have a dominant side. So it's good to take the time at the beginning to really work on getting your horse as supple as possible in both directions. For the less experienced rider who may have trouble with turns, put up a pair of cones where you need to turn into the exercise, then another pair of cones a few strides after the last jump to encourage straightness.

Once you and your horse are confidently and quietly trotting through the poles on the ground, add a cross-rail as Jump B. At first, it's fine if the horse simply trots over the cross-rail, especially if you are part of a less experienced pair. However, more seasoned pairs should land in the canter. To encourage your horse to do this, cue him to canter while going over Ground Pole A. This not only helps you work on your timing, it encourages your horse to make an actual jumping effort and land in the canter.

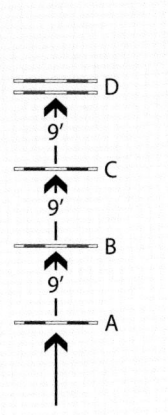

After you have done the simple cross-rail a few times, put in another cross-rail in the front standards of the oxer (Jump D). For the very green horse, this may be enough for one day, and that is completely fine! You can always come back the next day and add in the next few variations.

For pairs that are ready to move on, the next step is to change Jump D to an oxer, then change Jump B to a vertical.

Once you are comfortable doing this, raise Ground Pole C in the middle of the exercise. The easiest thing to do is to use white plastic blocks to raise the pole. But if you don't have access to those, use a cavalletti and simply raise it to the next level, or you can just get creative—as long as it is safe.

THE EXERCISES

From here, there are a few options depending on what you and your horse need to work on. If you have a horse that is really quick, start moving Ground Pole C closer to the vertical 6 inches at a time. This forces the horse to not jump past his distance, and instead land within a reasonable distance from Jump B, then put in a full stride before Jump D.

On the other hand, if your horse is a bit lazy, move Ground Pole C closer to Jump D to encourage him to stretch a bit in his one stride before taking off close to the base of the oxer.

Regardless of which direction you're moving the ground pole, you never want it closer than 6 feet from either the vertical or the oxer.

While every horse is different, rarely do I make the jumps in this exercise higher than 3 feet. There is so much footwork involved, especially at the end, that I am mostly interested in seeing horses concentrate on their footwork while keeping a relaxed back, and riders concentrate on their position without having to worry too much about the height of the fence. I am looking for the riders to really feel their hips move like flexible door hinges while their upper bodies remain tall with their arms relaxed and giving. ◆

EXERCISE

Traditional Gymnastic

EXPERT

Sharon White

of Last Frontier Farm in Summit Point, West Virginia

Bounces are such a great tool to help riders concentrate on their position over fences. And they are super for helping horses learn to balance themselves over a series of fences.

/ MATERIALS NEEDED

- 5 jump poles
- 5 sets of standards

/ SETUP

- You need 40 feet of space from Jump A to Jump E, which means that you need an arena that is at least 80 feet in length. If you do not have that much space, you can set this up along a diagonal or in a nearby field.

- Once everything is set up, place all jump poles on the ground.

▽ **About the expert:**

Sharon White is an accomplished international event rider and Level 4 ICP Instructor based at her own Last Frontier Farm in Summit Point, West Virginia. She is consistently successful at all levels of eventing, and emphasizes patience and empathy, along with discipline, in her training. She is known for her absolute dedication, perseverance, and cheerfulness in all circumstances, and most especially for her signature orange-and-white cross-country colors. ◆

www.lastfrontierfarm.com

/ WHY

This is one of my favorite exercises because it is useful for many different horses at many different levels. Equally important, it is a great exercise that allows riders to really concentrate on their body position.

Balance is the key to properly negotiating this grid. Your horse will learn how to slow down in the middle of an exercise and keep a balanced canter throughout. This will help you master the tools to keep the quality canter that will create clean jumping rounds.

I love this exercise because it really helps riders learn the value of rhythm, straightness, and the importance of staying soft through your elbows. As I mentioned earlier, the repetitive nature of the bounces allows riders to concentrate on their body position. More specifically, this particular exercise forces them to maintain strict upper body control.

Finally, this exercise teaches riders about their horses. For a lazier horse, it teaches the rider how to put her leg on through an entire exercise to help activate her horse's feet. For a more aggressive horse, it teaches the rider that she can soften her leg and use her upper body and core to control her horse.

/ HOW

Always start with all jump poles on the ground regardless of your level. You should trot through them a few times from either direction. Technically, the distance between the poles is a foot too long for trotting, so you should be getting two steps between each set of ground poles.

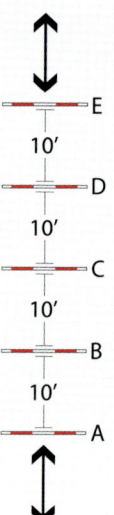

Keep trotting through until it is nice and smooth with no loss of rhythm. This may take you two turns through, it may take you 20; either way, your goal remains the same—steady rhythm and straightness. Next, pick up your canter with the same goal. Some young horses won't progress past the poles on the ground the first time through. That's okay! I believe ground rails are often overlooked in the education of young horses.

For a less experienced horse, start with Jump D as a small vertical. This leaves you with three poles before the jump and one after. You should trot through a few times until it is easy, and then do the same at the canter.

Once your horse is successfully picking his way through the ground poles and one jump, raise Jump B to a small vertical. This creates a nice one-stride with ground poles before, after, and between.

GRID PRO QUO / *Margaret Rizzo McKelvy* /

Next, raise Jump C to a small vertical so you have your first set of bounces.

When your horse is happily bouncing through this, add Jumps A and E. But if your horse is a little unsure of the first set of bounces, lower one side of each vertical to make it a little more inviting before putting them back up.

At any point, if you feel your horse has had enough, be sure to have one last positive ride through, then give him a pat and go for a hack. The point of this exercise is to build confidence, so it is better to quit early than to push the envelope and risk denting your horse's confidence.

For the more experienced horse, start by making Jump B and D verticals for an easy one-stride. Trot the first few times then move on to the canter. A more experienced horse will figure this exercise out rather quickly and you can add in Jump C for your first set of bounces, then Jumps A and E. More experienced horses can be challenged by playing with the height of the verticals. The idea is to keep changing the heights so that each time they come through it's the same distances but different heights. This is a great balancing exercise that also teaches your horse the proper shape to his body for jumping. Be sure to always start by raising something he has jumped a few times. I will often start by raising Jumps B, C and D, so that Jumps A and E are easy. Then try raising the Jumps A and E, and leaving Jumps B, C, and D low.

At most, the verticals should never get to over 3 feet 6 inches, and that would only be one of the verticals, which is reserved for upper-level horses. Five bounces are a lot of work!

If you have a horse that tends to rush, this is a great exercise! Horses can rarely rush through it without knocking a few rails. But if they are insistent on rushing, I start by putting up Jumps A and E and halting in the middle.

Or, if your horse tends to see the line of fences and take off, canter up to the bounces and halt before the first one. Either way, do your halt transition as many times as needed so that the horse is no longer anticipating and rushing at his fences.

Generally, you shouldn't have a problem with a horse stopping because you have built the exercise up piece by piece, giving him no reason to back off. If he is stalling out, you may have rushed building the exercise, so just take a step back. If you build it up piece by piece, you're building on your previous successes. The successful training of a horse comes from building on something that he understands. So taking a little time in the beginning rewards you in spades at the end. ◆

THE EXERCISES

EXPERT EXERCISE

Traditional Gymnastic

Kelley Williams

of A Bit Better Farm in Brookeville, Maryland

▽ About the expert:

A competitive upper-level event rider, Kelley Williams is known for her absolute dedication to her horses, her students, and her wonderfully supportive family. Kelley has developed A Bit Better Farm in Brookeville, Maryland, from a small family farm to a leading event facility. Kelley is a naturally gifted trainer and instructor who always seems to know what her pupils need, and she possesses an enviable amount of patience. She draws great gratification from her teaching and coaching, and firmly believes that she learns as much from her students as they do from her. ◆

www.abitbetterfarm.com

This is a great exercise for improving form for both horse and rider. All the poles encourage the horse to really look where he's putting his feet, and the repetitive nature of the distances allows the rider to concentrate on her position.

/ MATERIALS NEEDED

- 6 ground poles
- 9 jump poles
- 3 sets of standards

/ SETUP

- Set up the three jumps first and then place your ground poles. Once your distances are set, place all your jump poles on the ground.

- Be sure to double check all the distances and have a ground person on hand should your horse knock a ground pole out of place at any point.

GRID PRO QUO / *Margaret Rizzo McKelvy* /

/ WHY

This is a favorite grid of mine, both for teaching students and training horses, because it can be used to help horses and riders alike improve their form over fences. It encourages horses to think about where they place their feet as they jump through the line, as well as use their entire body more efficiently and correctly.

With so much to look at, it can be a bit of a mental puzzle for the horse. This makes the line particularly effective with a horse that tends to rush or get against your hand. The cross-rails combined with the vertical jumps act like balance poles, which help keep the horse straight as well as improve the action of both the front and hind limbs. Therefore, the grid can be a great workout for your equine partner, even if you are not ready to make your jumps very tall.

For the rider, this grid provides an opportunity to feel a horse that is properly straight and properly forward as a result of your leg. Without leg pressure, many horses slow down or shorten their stride through this line as they study the mental puzzle I mentioned earlier. While your horse is figuring out the puzzle, you have the responsibility of keeping the canter rhythm steady throughout, using leg pressure. This ultimately results in not only a more powerful jump, but a straighter horse as well. The repetition of two strides allows you to adjust your position and aids as you go through. I find this repetition really lets you feel the difference you can make in the way the line rides.

/ HOW

Depending on your and your horse's level of experience, you can begin in one of two ways.

For younger or less confident horses and less advanced riders, start with just Jump B and placement rails. When starting out, the jumps should be set to a little below your competition height.

You can warm up over this single jump a few times each direction at the trot. Pay close attention to maintaining a consistent rhythm in the trot as you apply leg to keep the horse at the center of the jump. Be sure to soften your rein, allowing him the chance to carry himself and use his neck and back.

Then move on to the canter, applying the same practices you did at the trot until you feel your horse can keep a steady rhythm to the middle of the jump on a straight-line approach and departure. I finish the exercise with the

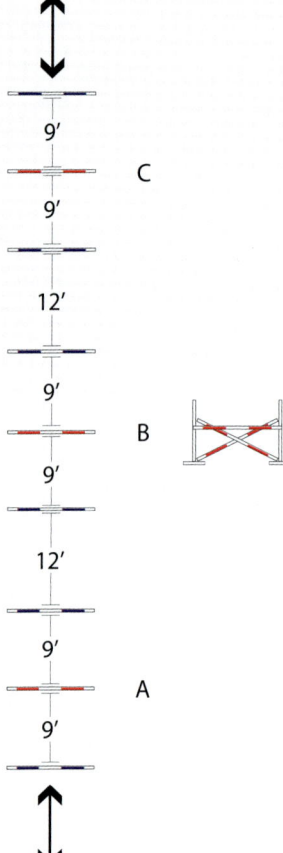

jumps set a hole or two higher than your normal competition height.

When you're ready, lower Jump B back to where you started and add Jump A or C along with its placement rails. At this point, you should only be approaching the jumps at the canter unless your horse has a strong tendency toward rushing, in which case you can trot in.

Once you and your horse are at ease with two jumps, add your final jump along with its placement rails. And if space allows for a fourth iteration of the distances, you can add that next, but I find three jumps fit nicely in my ring and are more than sufficient for the exercise to be useful.

For the more advanced horses, you can start with the entire grid in place. Just be sure to set the jumps (both verticals and cross-rails) very low so they are more like glorified cavalletti and will encourage the horse to think about his foot placement as he canters down the line.

Repeat the exercise in both directions until the horse can do it in a very steady rhythm.

Once you've cantered through the exercise successfully a few times, you have the choice of what do to next.

If your horse needs to work on his strength and ability to rock back to his hindquarters to jump, the best thing to do is raise the vertical rails one or two holes at a time, never going more than a few holes above the horse's current competition height, and going slowly enough to give him the chance to adjust his stride to the exercise as it gets harder.

As the jumps get taller the horse will feel the shortened distances a little more, requiring him

GRID PRO QUO / *Margaret Rizzo McKelvy* /

to jump more "up" than "at" the jumps. This can be quite a "heavy lifting" workout, which can cause fatigue fairly quickly, so I always take lots of walk breaks and am sure to end the session when my horse is tired. You are always smarter to end a session early than to push a horse to a place where he can no longer perform the task at hand successfully.

If you have a younger horse or one that tends to be slow with his front end, the best thing to do is raise the cross-rails, making the "opening" in the jumps smaller. By doing this, the cross-rails act more like "balance rails," helping to keep the horse at the center of the exercise and encouraging him to be more clever with his front end. ◆

EXPERT EXERCISE

Cavalletti and Coursework

Ryan Wood

of Woodstock Eventing in Cochranville, Pennsylvania

▽ **About the expert:**

An Australian native, Ryan Wood moved to the United States in 2008 and currently bases his Woodstock Eventing out of Cochranville, Pennsylvania. Ryan has competed at some of the world's premier events, including Adelaide CCI5*, Kentucky CCI5*, Fair Hill CCI4*, and more. In addition to Ryan's passion for riding, he enjoys seeing others succeed through lessons, coaching, and clinics. He takes great pride in developing horses and being a part of their journey, knowing that each horse has something unique to teach us. ◆

www.woodstockeventing.com

This is a great exercise for working on your coursework skills without putting unnecessary pounding on your horse's legs. This series of cavalletti will help you work on your horse's rideability and adjustability.

/ MATERIALS NEEDED

- 4 ground poles
- 4 cavalletti

/ SETUP

- This can be set up in your arena or jumping field.
- To start, leave your cavalletti on the lowest setting.

/ WHY

While this jumping exercise doesn't involve any actual jumps, I find that it is the perfect exercise

GRID PRO QUO / Margaret Rizzo McKelvy /

/ 204

to help my students and horses ride their courses better. I often find that once you start jumping a course, your horse can get on a roll and become a bit flat, which leads to his form dissipating a little bit. This exercise is all about rideability and adjustability, which are two ingredients to riding a clear and safe jumping course.

The key to this exercise is not the cavalletti themselves but being able to keep your horse on the aids and straight through the chute of jump poles on the ground. The short distance of 18 feet between the cavalletti really requires a horse to sit down and use his hind end. It also requires the rider to have her horse on the aids, with a clear connection between the inside leg to outside rein. As riders and horses progress through the levels, the challenge is to land after the last cavalletti, and leg-yield to either side before reaching the chute.

The best thing about this exercise is that it can be left up in your arena or jump field and worked into your ride several times a week. I sometimes flat a horse in a jump saddle and finish the session by going through this exercise a few times. Using cavalletti doesn't put a lot of wear and tear on the horse, so you can spend the time trying to perfect the exercise without worrying about pounding your horse's legs.

/ **HOW**

Depending on your level of riding, there are several ways you can start. For those at the 3-foot level or below, I recommend extending the distance to 21 feet, and starting with the cavalletti on their lowest height. For 3-foot level and above combinations, the 18 foot distance is perfectly appropriate.

Depending on your horse and your own experience level, you can either start with the cavalletti at their lowest height or start with them set up to the full height, which should be around 18 inches. The poles on the ground should be placed between four and six strides away from the cavalletti, depending on the level of the horse and rider. I would expect an upper-level horse to be able to complete a leg-yield within four strides, but I am okay with it taking six strides for lower-level pairs.

For the lower-level rider, the only goal should be to quietly canter through the exercise in balance with the horse in self-carriage. Horses are creatures of habit, so I try to repeat an exercise until they find it easy and natural. For the rider, I find that forcing someone to be really picky about the details while

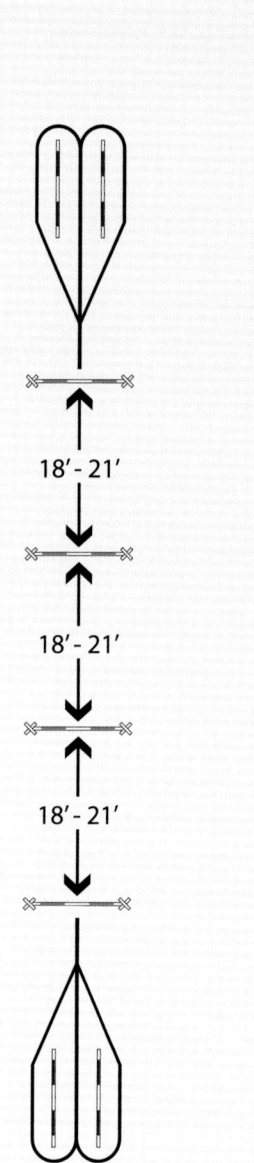

schooling will pay off at a horse show. Having the guide rails here forces the rider to be accurate and gives her something to aim for and work around. Then being able to do this exercise multiple times, and doing it as perfectly as possible, gives the rider confidence when she is faced with a similar situation at a horse show.

While I extend the distance between the cavalletti, and then the cavalletti and the "chute" between ground poles, I do still want riders at the lower-level to challenge themselves by asking their horse to canter through the cavalletti and then leg-yield away from the inside leg—so if you are cantering on the right lead, leg-yield away from your right leg to the left—before the chute, and then circling back to come through the chute in the opposite direction and over the cavalletti again.

For a slightly bigger challenge, leg-yield away from the outside leg—so if you are cantering on the right lead, you leg-yield away from your left leg to the right—before the chute, and then do a simple change of lead on the straight line before circling back to come through the chute and continuing on with your exercise.

When teaching, I always find it interesting to see what a rider thinks she is doing, versus what she is *actually* doing. It is not uncommon for a horse to run through the turns leaning on his inside shoulder. Without even realizing it, many riders will make this problem worse by relying on their inside rein to make the turn, without supporting the horse with their leg aids. This is where the rails on the ground come in handy, because it makes it obvious that you need to use more leg to make the leg-yield happen. I find

GRID PRO QUO / Margaret Rizzo McKelvy /

that this exercise really breaks things down, so that you can learn to put your leg on more in a low-stress environment.

When I'm schooling this exercise on my own horses, I am looking for a few specific things as I work through the cavalletti. For a horse that canters into the exercise, but then fumbles through the cavalletti, I break the exercise down a little bit. For me, everything I do with horses is about progression. So, for a horse that is struggling a bit, I start by cantering over the end cavalletti on their own a few times. I often then take out one of the end cavalletti momentarily, and canter over two cavalletti before adding the third one back in, and then canter down the line and continue with the exercise.

On the other hand, I will sometimes have a horse that is a bit too bold and tries to rush through the cavalletti, and even bounce through the distance. Again, I believe that repetition is the key to success, so I will simply extend the distance out to 21 feet to make it a very clear one-stride. And once the horse understands, I close in the distance gradually until I am back to the 18 foot distance.

Occasionally, I have a horse that is insistent on rushing, and while some might think that you need to complicate the exercise to get the horse's attention, I like to break the exercise down to its basics in order to make it very clear what I am expecting. Depending on the horse, I will either take away a few of the cavalletti, or I simply start by trotting into the exercise, letting him land and canter away, but then come back to the trot before turning to come back through the chute. I repeat this as many times as necessary, until the exercise starts to have a calming effect on the horse, instead of revving him up. ◆

There are so many people who have played a part in the creation of this book, and I simply must put my gratitude on paper. Firstly, to the United States Eventing Association, for giving *Grid Pro Quo* a start as a column in their magazine. To Trafalgar Square Books, for bringing my vision to life with this book. And to all the professionals who let me share their favorite exercises in these pages. To my husband Scott, for always supporting this crazy horse habit of mine and for always encouraging me to reach for the stars. To my parents, for signing my sister Katherine and me up for lessons as kids. To my friends, for always being there to encourage and support my ambitious ideas. To all my instructors over the years, for providing such expert coaching—I would not have been able to achieve any of my riding goals without you. And lastly to my horses: to Lissell for taking care of me for many years and keeping me safe, and to Stilts for helping me learn how to truly fly and dance. ◆

ACKNOWLEDGMENTS